History **&** Guide

BERWICK
UPON TWEED

Jim Walker

Herring boats alongside Berwick Quay in 1904. The boat with the sails fully hoisted is a 'Fifie'. At this time Berwick was a major herring fishing port.

History & Guide

BERWICK
UPON TWEED

Jim Walker

TEMPUS

The Buttermarket at the rear of the Town Hall, from where there is an entrance to an intriguing coffee house adapted from disused jail cells.

First published 2001, reprinted 2003

Tempus Publishing Limited
The Mill, Brimscombe Port,
Stroud, Gloucestershire, GL5 2QG

© Jim Walker, 2001

British Library Cataloguing in Publication Data.
A catalogue record for this book is available from the British Library.

ISBN 0 7524 2262 6

Typesetting and origination by Tempus Publishing Limited
Printed in Great Britain by Midway Colour Print, Wiltshire

CONTENTS

ACKNOWLEDGEMENTS

In the production of this book, I am greatly indebted to the following, who have helped me, either by the loaning of photographs or the furnishing of information, or by granting me the facilities to take photographs:

Mr D. Anderson, Mrs L. Bankier (Borough Archivist), Mrs A. Bell, Mr E. Bowes, Mr I. Bruce, Mr and Mrs A. Burn, Mr F.M. Cowe, Mr P.E. Dixon, Mr C. Green (Borough Museum Director), Miss M.A. Gregg, Mrs B. Herdman, Revd A. Hughes, Mr T. Johnson, Miss A. Lee, Mrs B. Lough, Mr B. Page, Mrs E. Rathbone, Mrs B. Ross, Mrs L. Suthren.

Last but not least my heartfelt thanks to my wife Connie, without whose help and support this book would not have been possible, also a special thank-you to my niece Sheila Scott, whose efficiency and fortitude in the face of my typing requirements has been remarkable.

My grateful thanks to all.

Jim Walker

Looking towards Cumberland Bastion from Brass Bastion, showing the long stretch of curtain wall. On the right can be seen a section of the original cobbled sentry walk. The sentry walks were buried when the huge mounds of earth called cavaliers were added in 1639.

PREFACE

Many travellers have written (favourably and unfavourably) about Berwick upon Tweed, the earliest being the unknown chronicler who accompanied Edward I on his journeys. He provides us with an authentic account of the storming of 'Barwyk upon Twede' in 1296, when the 'Hammer of the Scots' unleashed his full fury on the town.

Some three and a half centuries later, a French traveller in 1661 wrote of Berwick having open areas with great fountains and many great palaces, and that 'by walking over Barwyk I discovered it to be one of the greatest and most beautiful towns in England'. Robert Burns was dismissive in 1787 when he described it as 'an idle town rudely picturesque'. He seemed to be more concerned regarding the impression he had made on Lord Errol whom he met while walking on the walls.

Of all the accounts of travellers to Berwick, however, the one which seems to me to capture the essence of this remarkable town is that of George Borrow. A traveller and philosopher, George Borrow wrote in his largely autobiographical masterpiece *Lavengro* about seeing Berwick for the first time when he was a youth of eleven. His father's regiment, the Norfolk Militia, were marching to Edinburgh from Norwich in 1813 and stopped over in Berwick. As a captain, Borrow senior would have been permitted to have his family accompany him, and so the young Borrow writes: 'It was a beautiful morning of early spring, small white clouds were floating in the heaven, occasionally veiling the countenance of the sun, whose light, as they retired would again burst forth, coursing like a racehorse over the scene – and a goodly scene it was! Before me, across the water on an eminence, stood a white old city surrounded with lofty walls, above which rose the tops of tall houses, with here and there a church or steeple. To my right hand was a long and massive bridge, with many arches and of antique architecture which traversed the river. The river was a noble one, the broadest that I had hitherto seen'.

He observed the salmon fishers (probably working the old Pool fishery, situated on the south side of the river between the old and new road bridges), and compared the Danube, the Rhine and the Tiber unfavourably with the beauty of the River Tweed. As he crossed the bridge into Berwick he said of the town: 'but now I have seen it I shall not soon forget it!'

CHAPTER 1
Prehistoric to the Dark Ages

Berwick and the Tweed estuary lie in an area known to geologists as the Northumberland Trough. Some 200 to 300 million years ago it was part of a delta, and with the sea periodically flooding over the delta, various depositions of limestone, shale, sandstone and coal were formed. This span of time is known as the Carboniferous Period, and it is when the coal seams around Berwick were laid down. These seams, albeit shallow, were worked round Berwick and Scremerston for hundreds of years, finishing finally in 1959. Fossils from this period are to be found in the rocks along the coast, and a striking example of a fossilized tree trunk from this time can be seen in the cliffs at the far end of Spittal. The fossilized remains of small marine animals (brachiopods) and corals, as well as evidence of the Lepidodrendron tree, make it possible to build up a geological history and geography of the area.

Fossilized branch of a Lepidodendron tree at Spittal.

Further down the coast at Howick Bay are traces of footprints, caused by an amphibian crawling out of the water on to damp sand. A further flooding of sand and water has preserved them and these are some of the oldest footprints in Britain, dating back more than 200 million years to an age known as the Palaeozoic era.

About 10,000 years ago, the last ice age which had covered the land with vast areas of sheet ice had receded. Due to rising temperatures, the ice began to melt and at that time, the islands we now call Britain were linked to the continental land mass of what we now know as Europe. A valley, many metres below the present Tweed estuary, was formed either by ice or water, its route to the sea being through the west end of Spittal, rather than the winding loop the river takes today between Sandstell Point and the pier. The sea level at that time was some 20m below what it is now.

Mankind has existed in Europe for some 700,000 or 800,000 years, but it was only perhaps some 12,000 years ago that re-settlement of humans began in Britain. Rising levels of the warmer seas about 8,000 years ago, coupled with land movements after being freed from the weight of ice, resulted in the separation of the British Isles from continental Europe. Thereafter, visitors to Britain by necessity had to arrive in boats, even though they might be only primitive coracles, dug-outs or even rafts of logs.

On land, trees and shrubby plants would have been spreading for some thousands of years; by 5,000 years ago, deciduous forests would have been covering much of the Tweed basin. At this time, the people who inhabited this area would be hunter-gatherers, who would not be

The last of the hunter-gatherers (!) in the form of a poacher at Hallowstell, Spittal. The net is thrown and (inset) a salmon is caught.

unlike the Australian Aborigines of today, in that they subsisted on the hunting of wild animals, fishing, and the gathering and eating of roots, plants and fruits.

On the estuarial banks of the Tweed, it is likely there would have been a cluster of hunter-gatherers, for there would be fish to be caught, and shellfish to be gathered. Later, a more advanced society would use nets and river traps made from woven branches to catch salmon and trout. Small groups of hunter-gatherers would travel up river at certain seasons, where they would settle for a period at favourable sites which were often at the junction of rivers.

Later on, settlements developed and construction of burial mounds began, suggesting some form of developing society. The burying of their dead must have had extreme significance, and to inter their dead in elaborate graves marking them with cairns would necessarily involve quite heavy work, and a measure of organized labour. We have the evidence of flint arrow-heads and stone axes for the existence of hunter-gatherers, and later we find beakers in the graves, suggesting a belief that worldly possessions were required for the deceased on their journey after death. Stone axes were sometimes deposited with beakers, and it is known that axes were imported to the area; many came from Cumbria where at one axe factory the debris of 75,000 axe heads has been found.

Some 4,000 years ago, after the span of time now referred to as the Neolithic (New Stone Age) period, metal began to be introduced. This was the start of the Bronze Age, when settlements became more permanent, and boundaries were made. Farming methods were established with domesticated animals, such as sheep and goats, being herded. Previously, wild animals such as the aurochs would have roamed free, and a close relative of the aurochs can be seen today at Chillingham Park where the unique Chillingham wild cattle survive. Much bigger than modern cattle, they are white with dark eyes, black muzzles and hooves; it may be that as a herd of wild cattle, they were corralled around the thirteenth century as a source of food.

The people who used beakers have been given the name of the Beaker People or Beaker Folk, but they would not have recognized themselves by an identity such as this. Nevertheless it is known that they began to arrive in Britain about 2000 BC. Physically, they were tall, robust, round-headed people, and different to the more slightly built, long-headed Neolithic types. That the beakers were prized possessions is undoubted, for they had elaborate decorations incised on them. The beakers may have played a part in ceremonial rites, or they

Wild cattle at Chillingham.

may have been special drinking vessels for occasions when they would be filled with a type of beer. No doubt Bronze Age man and woman would have times when celebrations were in order – perhaps when the days began to lengthen after the winter solstice on 22 December.

A site which should be visited is Roughting Linn, reached from the Berwick-Wooler road. This, if you are receptive, can give you a unique impression of a Bronze Age religious experience. Here, there is a great variety of carving on a large outcrop of sandstone, which lies east of a later defensive fort. These carvings, known as 'cup and ring' marks, are very much a part of the history of this area. These unique symbols are found in their greatest number in North and West Spain, the British Isles and central Switzerland, but Northumberland is among the richest areas for rock carvings in Britain. Some of these carvings have been found on the underside of cist lids (i.e. stone coffins with slabs of stone for lids) as well as those cut into the soft fell sandstone. What was their purpose and why did Bronze Age man spend time picking at the rock with primitive tools to make such intricate patterns? No-one can tell, and although there are almost as many theories as there are carvings, it is perhaps best to recognize that we will never know. Whatever the reasons, they must have been very compelling and important to their way of life as individuals and communities. There is a lovely waterfall at Roughting Linn (the name means cataract/pool), as well as recesses in the sandstone at the head of the ravine, and as water has been associated with ritual from time immemorial, it is not hard to imagine primitive man engaging in rituals here. Certainly, on the shortest day of the year, the sun can penetrate to the top of the ravine, which surely must have seemed magical.

Beaker (c. 2000 BC) found in a cist at Murton, three miles from Berwick, and now in the Berwick Museum. At one time this belonged to Dr Johnston, founder of the Berwickshire Naturalists' Club.

Cup and ring marks at Roughting Linn.

The standing stone circle at Duddo after a winter storm.

Just 4 miles south west of Roughting Linn at the village of Milfield is a reconstruction of a Neolithic henge. Several henges have been recorded across the area of Milfield Plain. These circular monuments are made up of an inner ditch and an earthen mound surrounding it, with one or two entrances. They may have been ritual places, and it is possible they were associated with the imposing mountain of Yeavering Bell, for the alignment of these henges seem to lead naturally to that feature, suggesting a processional route.

Some 6 miles north of Milfield, near Duddo, is the best of the standing stone circles in the area. There are five large upright stones set in a circle on a rise in the field. Obviously a type of ceremonial monument, it would appear to have sacred significance for there are cup marks on some of the stones. Probably when first constructed, there would have been more stones, forming a complete circle, but it is astonishing that any are left considering the thousands of years they have been there.

There are no brochs in Northumberland, but if you fancy a short trip over the Border, there is one in Berwickshire. Brochs are circular stone towers, mainly found in Orkney and Shetland. They have double walls enclosing apartments on more than one level. Twenty miles from Berwick near Abbey St Bathans (NT 772603) the remains of a large, stone broch is situated on the site of a hill fort. Edin's Hall, as it is known, is an impressive structure, and although its name may be derived from King Edwin of Northumbria (sixth century), it was probably built at least 500 years before he reigned. However, it is not beyond the bounds of possibility that the broch may have been occupied for centuries, right up to the time of Edwin.

A transitional period between 1000 BC and 650 BC saw the Bronze Age merge into the Iron Age, so called because of the widespread smelting and use of iron. Hill forts and hilltop settlements were built in profusion in Northumbria at this time. The need for these may have been due to a more unsettled and warlike world, for they are so numerous that they must have been essential for the social and military structure of the period. Yeavering Bell has been mentioned, but another impressive hill fort is at Old Bewick (NT 075216), just off the Wooler to Morpeth road. Here multiple ramparts and ditches surround a double hill fort, and although slippage of earth has softened the lines of the ditches, the depth of the excavation is still formidable.

Later, these hill forts would assume more of a non-defensive character, when the Roman campaigns brought their imperial standards to the north. The area which later became known as Northumbria was populated by a tribe known as the Votadini, who were thought by the Romans to be more co-operative than the tribe to the west called the Selgovae. The Romans built a bridge over the Tyne and roads running north, but there is scanty evidence of the Roman period in the Berwick area. A road has existed since Roman times, subsequently named The Devil's Causeway, which runs for 60 miles from Corbridge, three miles south of Hadrian's Wall. Though little can be seen now, the road has been well documented and it possibly crossed the Tweed upstream from Berwick near West Ord to march on up the Bound Road, passing near the ruined castle of Edrington and on to Mordington in a straight line.

This modern road south of Lowick is on the line of the Roman road or Devil's Causeway.

A map of 1769 showing the line of the Devil's Causeway. It also shows Witches' Knowe between Marshall Meadows and Mordington. In 1929 a Mr Craw said his father knew a man who when a boy, had been told by a very old woman that she could remember being carried as a child to see a witch burned on the Knowe. She said 'when the fire was lit, the crazed old woman held out her skinny hands to warm them at the blaze'.

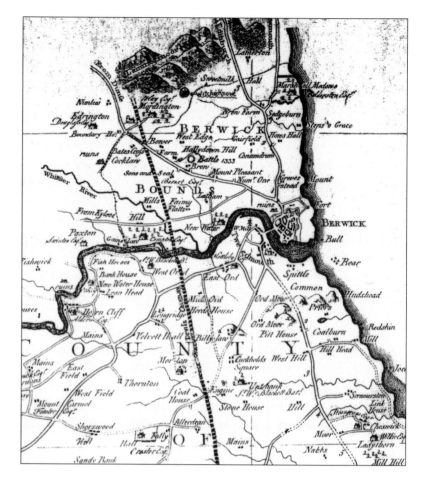

A Roman fort may have been sited near the reservoir at Sunnyside, and aerial photography has suggested such. An excavation in 1946 found some third-century pottery which seemed to confirm the existence of a fort. A spur of the Roman road may have gone down to the river, somewhere near Tweedmouth church, where the Tweed could have been fordable at low tide. Certainly it is unlikely that the Romans would not have been aware of the advantages of a haven for their navy, and the possibility of using the Tweed as a arterial waterway to the important military base at Trimontium (Three Mountains) near Melrose.

In the era of Roman Britannia, the northern half of the British Isles, called Caledonia or Alba (now Scotland), was inhabited by three separate, if overlapping, ethnic groups. The first, in the north, most commonly called Picts, were non-Celtic or lightly Celticized tribes who existed before the arrival of the Celtic people around 600 BC. In the south, there were two types of Celtic groups known as 'P' Celts and 'Q' Celts. (The name derives from a feature of their languages, where words which began with 'P' in one language often began with 'Q' in the other.) Border tribes like the Votadini were the kinsfolk of the 'P' Celts, and they were called (in their own speech) Gododdin.

There may be a folk memory of this time, for part of a poem which came to light two centuries ago speaks of Gilligacus, which is very like the name of a leader Calgacus mentioned by Tacitus the Roman historian.

Sin the days of Gilligacus
There's been fishers on the Tweed
Sin the Romans came to wrack us
And consume our ancient seed
A castle strong has been to back us
On the tap o' yon brae head.

The rhyme is supposed to refer to Berwick Castle, but there is no evidence to back this up.

Roman roads in Scotland were marked with milestones and the distances shown were reckoned to and from Trimontium. Eildon Hill North was a signal station, and with mirror or fire, messages could be relayed down the Tweed Valley to Berwick, for the Eildon Hills are a prominent landmark in the fairly flat landscape viewed from Berwick.

As the Romans liked their wine, large numbers of supply ships would come from the Mediterranean or Gaul, and oil would also be imported. Other bulky materials would also come by ship, and it seems logical to think of the mouth of the river Tweed as being a port, where goods could be transhipped into shallow-draught vessels for the journey up the Tweed to the Roman garrison.

At this time, forests of oak, ash and birch covered most of the hill slopes, and much of the lower-lying ground, with little or no drainage, would have been boggy. The native tribes had a comparatively high degree of civilization. They herded horses, oxen and sheep and cultivated wheat and barley. They had wheeled transport and lived in small oval enclosures containing huts of wattle and daub, thatched with straw. They traded with their conquerors and Roman coinage was used as the local currency, so that in effect this area would best be described as a Roman protectorate.

In AD 410 came the collapse of Roman rule, after a period of 350 years during which they had ruled their colony of Britain with a fair measure of success, for Britain was a relatively prosperous province of the Roman Empire. Anglo-Saxons who came from what is now Denmark and the land of Saxony at the mouth of the Rhine were attacking, and appeals to Rome for help were of no avail. Thereafter, for more than 200 years the Anglo-Saxons continued settling and forming kingdoms, and it is in this period that Berwick would have first been recognized and named.

The Romanized Britons were submerged by the invaders, although in the north, the Picts and Scots resisted, and indeed the Picts were aggressors who raided the south by sea in this period. At the time the Angles were flooding into this area in the fifth century, others were settling further south, their main town being what is now York (Eboracum). Bamburgh was the capital of the Angles in our part of Northumbria which was called Bernicia, and eventually in the late seventh century, the two rival Angle dynasties were combined and Bernicia stretched from the Humber to the Forth. The first king of Bernicia was Ida the Flamebearer who ruled from 547 to 560 from the rock of Bamburgh.

Some time before the beginning of the sixth century, the heroic figure of King Arthur (he of the Round Table) makes an appearance. Historians are still arguing about Arthur, whether he really did exist and whether he led the resistance against the Anglo-Saxon invaders. It is likely that a British warlord did exist, and that he fought many successful battles against the intruders who were trying to expand their kingdoms. It is quite possible that eight out of ten

LINE	DATE	SCOTLAND. RULERS	DATE	ENGLAND. RULERS	LINE
	83AD-211	ROMANS.	43AD-410	ROMANS	
	211-843	PICTS, SCOTS BRITONS & ANGLES	410-650	DARK AGES ANGLO-SAXONS	
ALPIN	843-859	KENN. MACALPIN	650-830	HEPTARCHY.	
	859-1005	APPOINTED SUCCESSORS	830-839	EGBERT	SAXON AND VIKING
	1005-1034	MALCOLM II	871-899	ALFRED THE GREAT	
DUNKELD	1034-1040	DUNCAN I	924-940	ATHELSTANE	
	1040-1058	MACBETH AND LULACH (1 YEAR)	1042-1066	EDWARD THE CONFESSOR.	
	1058-1094	MALCOLM III & DUNCAN II (& DONALD BAN (1 YEAR))	1066	HAROLD.	
	1094-1097	DONALD & EDMUND.	1066-1087	WILLIAM THE CONQUEROR.	
	1097-1107	EDGAR.	1087-1100	WILLIAM II (RUFUS)	NORMAN
	1107-1124	ALEXANDER I	1100-1135	HENRY I	
CANMORE	1124-1153	DAVID I	1135-1154	STEPHEN	
	1153-1165	MALCOLM IV	1154-1189	HENRY II	
	1165-1214	WILLIAM (THE LION)	1189-1199	RICHARD I	
	1214-1249	ALEXANDER II	1199-1216	JOHN.	PLANTAGENETS AND ANGEVINS
	1249-1286	ALEXANDER III	1216-1272	HENRY III	
	1286-1290	MARGARET	1272-1307	EDWARD I HAMMER OF THE SCOTS	
	1292-1296	JOHN BALLIOL	1307-1327	EDWARD II	
BRUCE	1296-1306	UNDER ENGLISH RULE EDWARD I	1327-1377	EDWARD III	
	1306-1329	ROBERT BRUCE	1377-1399	RICHARD II	
	1329-1371	DAVID II	1399-1413	HENRY IV	LANCASTER AND YORK.
	1371-1390	ROBERT II	1413-1422	HENRY V	
	1390-1406	ROBERT III	1422-1461	HENRY VI	
	1406-1437	JAMES I	1461-1483	EDWARD IV (& V)	
STEWART	1437-1460	JAMES II	1483-1485	RICHARD III	
	1460-1488	JAMES III	1485-1509	HENRY VII	
	1488-1513	JAMES IV KILLED AT FLODDEN.	1509-1547	HENRY VIII	
	1513-1542	JAMES V	1547-1553	EDWARD VI	TUDOR
	1542-1567	MARY (QUEEN OF SCOTS)	1553-1558	MARY I. (BLOODY)	
	1567-1603	JAMES VI ---	1558-1603	ELIZABETH I.	

1603-1625	JAMES I & VI	
1625-1649	CHARLES I	
1649-1660	CROMWELL	
1660-1685	CHARLES II	STUART
1685-1688	JAMES II & VII	
1689-1702	WILLIAM & MARY.	
1702-1714	ANNE	
1714-1727	GEORGE I	
1727-1760	GEORGE II	
1760-1820	GEORGE III	GEORGIAN.
1820-1830	GEORGE IV	
1830-1837	WILLIAM IV.	
1837-1901	VICTORIA	
1901-1910	EDWARD VII	
1910-1936	GEORGE V	WINDSOR.
1936-1952	GEORGE VI	
1952-	ELIZABETH.	

Rulers of England and Scotland.

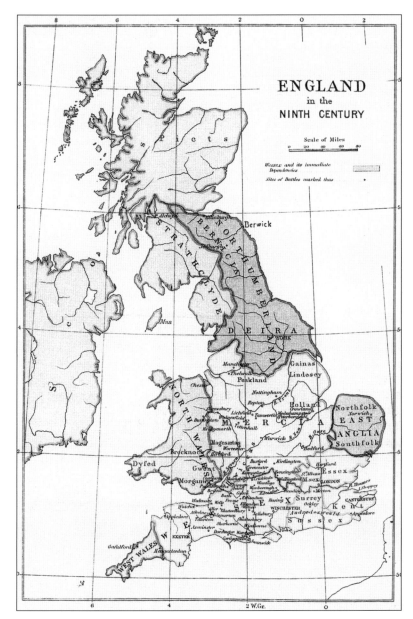

ENGLAND
in the
NINTH CENTURY

Scale of Miles

Wessex and its immediate Dependencies

Sites of Battles marked thus

The vast area of Northumberland is clearly seen in this map of England in the ninth century, extending as it does from the Humber to the Forth.

battles fought by Arthur were in the area now known as the Borders, and a good case for Arthur having his stronghold at Roxburgh Castle (just 20 miles from Berwick) has been made by Alistair Moffat in his book *Arthur and the Lost Kingdoms*.

Whatever the truth of the matter, one thing for sure is that once the shield of the Roman legions was removed, there was incessant warfare for centuries. Despite discrepancies in dates, the powerful folktales persisted about this warlike hero, and by the twelfth century minstrels all over Europe were telling of Arthur's exploits. If Arthur did fight his battles in northern Northumbria and the Borders, he had a fertile area in which to recruit, for Northumbrians were recognized as a mixture of different races who were stubborn and rebellious, and woe betide visitors to the area who did not come in the shape of armed expeditions!

Nevertheless, from the seventh to the ninth centuries, there was a confederacy of Anglo-Saxon kingdoms, seven in total. Northumbria, as it was now named, had great influence in this Heptarchy, primarily because of the dominance of the Northumbrian Church with its great cultural traditions centred at Lindisfarne. Christianity was introduced here in AD 635 by St Aidan at the instigation of the King of Bernicia, Oswald, a Christian convert. Missionaries spread out from Lindisfarne, including one St Boisil who is credited with having set up a preaching station near where the present Tweedmouth church stands, and which is dedicated to St Bartholomew and St Boisil. It should be remembered that Christianity had been introduced to this area by the Romans, but probably with limited permanence, for just a century after the Romans left, the Anglo-Saxons, who were pagans, were penetrating as far as the Cheviots.

One might be forgiven for thinking that with the coming of Christianity, life would have been less violent and brutish for the inhabitants of Britain, but as ever, wars continued between the various kingdoms, especially those of the south. In Northumbria, the pursuits of peace were gaining ascendancy, but this was not to last, and the people were blissfully unaware of the horrors to come from the plundering raids of 'the people from the North'.

These Scandinavian raiders, usually referred to as Vikings, began their raids in 787, and in 793 when 'dire portents appeared over Northumbria and sorely frightened the people', the worst was expected. Whirlwinds, lightning, dragons and famine as portents were bad enough, but when these were followed by Norse invaders burning the settlements of Lindisfarne and killing the monks, the inhabitants' cups were full and running over with misery. This raid of 793 was the first recorded account of a series of raids on the coast of the North Sea, and many such raids have probably not been recorded. Legend has it that the Norsemen, perhaps driven off course, landed at Spittal. These plundering raids continued until 867 when the Vikings with their very efficient longships and their fearsome warriors sacked York. Effectively this ended the domination of the ancient kingdom of Northumbria, which was reduced in area to the land between the Tyne and

A sandstone slab found at Lindisfarne showing seven warriors thought to represent Vikings. It dates from the late ninth or early tenth centuries.

A cargo ship loading barley in Tweedmouth Docks. In the eighteenth century, Berwick was one of the principal grain ports in the UK and grain is still one of the main exports.

the Tweed. In 875 under Halfdan, the Norsemen burnt and destroyed the whole district between the Tyne and Tweed, and the Lindisfarne community left in haste with their treasures, the holy relics of St Cuthbert and the Lindisfarne Gospels. At this time the Norsemen did not settle in the lands they had ravaged.

Berwick is mentioned in some early writings as being in existence in 833 when Oseth, King of the Danes, is supposed to have 'aryved at Berwick in the Water of Twede', also later in that century when two Danes, Inguar and Ubba, landed at Berwick looking for revenge for the supposed murder of a Danish prince. Both these accounts may or may not be true, but undoubtedly Berwick would have existed as a settlement. Its name shows its Anglo-Saxon origins, being a settlement trading in barley – from 'bere' (barley) and 'wic' (village).

By this time, though, the Danes were settling in the area and probably taking over the existing farms. They may even have set up defensive points, and Berwick with its haven would have been recognized as a place to hold. York, however, was seen as the main centre of the area.

A representational Viking warrior in the English Heritage Priory Museum on Holy Island shows the distinctive Norseman's helmet.

As time went on, the invaders became integrated and Anglicized. Some became Christian and began to speak English, and the territory which their armies controlled became known as the Danelaw. York's Danish overlord, Sygtrygg the Squint-eyed, married the sister of the King of Wessex, Athelstan, and accepted Christianity, but subsequently his largely heathen subjects forced him to renounce both bride and religion. Marching north, Athelstan took York and killed his squint-eyed brother-in-law. Later, in 934, Athelstan moved his army north again, stopping at Chester-le-Street to pay homage at the shrine of St Cuthbert. His fleet would have passed by the bay of Berwick and his army would have marched through or near Berwick. The northern kings surrendered and Athelstan was in effect King of Britain.

In the autumn of 937 Athelstan fought the Norsemen and their allies, the Scots, at the battle of Brunanburh, which may have been in the southern part of Northumbria, or again it may have been Liverpool or Glasgow! No one knows, but it was one of the bloodiest battles ever fought in history, and it was known thereafter as the 'Great Battle', paralleling the 1914-1918 war which is known today as the 'Great War'. Athelstaneford near Haddington, some 35 miles north of Berwick, perhaps received its name from some association with the great Saxon king.

Northumbria, in the face of sudden vicissitudes of greatness and decay over the centuries, survived and it must be acknowledged that this northern land had been a significant force in the evolution of the British Isles. Its warriors and its missionaries played their part, the missionaries and saints gave us a new form of poetic literature – the Lindisfarne Gospels – and its warriors were responsible for forging a loose political unity, which was the beginning of England and Scotland as we now know them.

The mists of uncertainty now sweep in and Berwick, such as it was, would no doubt see and suffer marauders and warring armies, but it is not noted in any annals until the time of Malcolm II of Scotland. Malcolm fought the Northumbrian army at Carham (which is today in the Borough of Berwick), sometime about 1018. Malcolm's victory allowed him to claim the Tweed as a Scottish river and, by inference, Berwick also fell under his domination.

At this time, King Cnut (Canute), one of the last Danish rulers of England and also King of Denmark and Norway, demanded recompense from Malcolm II of Scotland for his annexation of the area down to the River Tweed. Subsequently Cnut received the homage of Malcolm II. Later, Malcolm's grandson, Duncan, tried to extend the Scottish boundary further south, but was defeated at Durham in 1039. Retreating to Berwick, he fitted out a fleet of eleven warships, and set sail northwards to go to the aid of Moddan, ruler of Orkney and Caithness. This was the Duncan who subsequently was assassinated by Macbeth in 1040.

It is worthy of note that Berwick at this time was capable of fitting out a fleet of eleven warships. Even though the ships may not all have been built in Berwick there must have been shipyards in existence, and all the ancillary trades: rope-makers, mast- and block-makers, sail-makers, coopers and victuallers. Almost 800 years later, warships were being built in Berwick for the Royal Navy at the time of the Napoleonic Wars, and when shipbuilding stopped in Berwick in 1979, an industry which had been carried on for 1,000 years ceased to exist.

Macbeth ruled for seventeen years and under him the north and south of Scotland were welded together, and for the first time became a recognizable nation. He had an enemy, however, in the form of Malcolm, son of Duncan, who had been assassinated by Macbeth. Malcolm wanted revenge for the murder of his father, but more importantly, he wanted to regain his hereditary right to the throne of Scotland. Berwick was again an assembly port for Malcolm's naval expeditionary force, and eventually he succeeded in his efforts, being crowned Malcolm III in 1058. He reigned for thirty-five years, thus consolidating the Kingdom of Scotland, which of course included Berwick. Not content with ruling over Scotland, he attacked Northumbria four times during his reign, trying to extend his kingdom and the border line down to the River Tyne. On a fifth raid into Northumbria, he was killed at Alnwick in 1093.

The master scribe Eadfrith wrote the Lindisfarne Gospels and the beautifully illuminated manuscripts are held in the British Museum. A virtual display of the Gospels can be seen in the visitors' centre at Holy Island.

Pilgrimages to Holy Island over the sands have been made for more than 1,000 years. There is a causeway which floods with each tide and can trap unwary visitors who have to take refuge in boxes built on stilts.

CHAPTER 2

Golden Years

Four years later, after Malcolm was killed, Malcolm's son Edgar was crowned king with the aid and support of the English King William Rufus (William II, son of the Conqueror). Berwick is mentioned at this time as 'the noble village of Berwick', being subject of a gift to the Bishop of Durham (i.e. a gift of the rents and revenues under feudal tenure). This gift was Edgar's thanks for help given by Rufus, enabling him to gain the crown of Scotland. That Berwick has always occupied a unique position is underlined by this action, for it was a Scottish possession, yet here it (i.e. its revenues) was being gifted to the Bishop of Durham. However, it would appear that the King changed his mind soon thereafter, and revoked the gift, having suffered a slight by the Bishop of Durham.

Edgar died in 1107 and his brother Alexander the Fierce then became ruler of the North of Scotland, while David his younger brother ruled in the south, viz. the Lothians and Cumbria. David became overall King of Scotland in 1124 following the death of Alexander. David had been brought up in England, and had received a Norman education, and was Prince of Cumbria in his own right.

In 1998 work on a housing development to the west of Berwick Castle uncovered human remains. After careful archaeological investigation by the University of Newcastle, the foundations of a medieval church (possibly that of the lost parish church of St Mary in Bondington) were exposed, as well as these grave slabs. Bondington was a separate parish to the north west of Berwick, and the church was probably abandoned in the fourteenth century. When Alexander III was killed in 1286, requiem masses were sung for his soul in the church of St Mary the Virgin, Bondington.

The Norman influence over Scotland was powerful, and increasingly the ruling Scottish dynasty was three-quarters non-native, and could be described as French. David was King of Scots and a brother of the Queen of England, wife of Henry I. His reign was constructive and brought benefits to Scotland, not least those of a cultural aspect. He founded abbeys; the first one was at Selkirk, which later moved to Kelso, no doubt because the weather was better and the soil was richer. These Benedictine monks were well endowed with possessions, including property in Berwick. Also, in 1130 King David gave the church of St Mary in Berwick to the monks of Coldingham. About this time a burgess of Berwick, who was Flemish, was transferred to St Andrews to help in the setting up of the machinery of a burgh, and to become its provost.

Berwick must therefore have been a burgh for some time before, and was a royal burgh along with Roxburgh. It is tempting to think of a period in the past to be a golden age, for it is a human failing to be nostalgic about the 'good old days'. Nevertheless, about this time, an era began which even cautious historians would say led to a golden age for Berwick.

David I ruled until 1153, and for the most part his reign was peaceful, but he was not above warring to increase his power and extend his kingdom. Marching south in 1138, with a motley army comprising Normans, Flemings, Germans, Northumbrians (which no doubt included some Berwickers), Cumbrians, Scots, English and men from Galloway, Teviotdale and the Lothians, he met the English near Northallerton and was defeated. Fighting on the English side was a knight of England, Robert de Brus, an ancestor of Robert the Bruce who would become King of Scotland. Nevertheless, despite his defeat, David by some adroit negotiations finished up by gaining the whole of Northumbria, the Scottish boundary being extended south to the River Tees. To be fair, David did have a claim by marriage to Northumbria, but it was still a good outcome from a defeat at arms!

The population in this area, though small, was increasing and David pursued an active policy of encouraging immigrants from the Low Countries, especially Flanders, and a large colony became settled in Berwick. By encouraging trade in his royal burgh of Berwick, he helped to increase the prosperity of Scotland generally, and made his own position more secure against any aspiring contenders for his throne. David re-founded Melrose Abbey, and under the leadership of his stepson who was second abbot there, it prospered commercially (for religious foundations were the powerhouses of commerce). Large quantities of wool were produced from the flocks of sheep owned by the Abbey, and this along with hides and other goods were taken to Berwick and from there were shipped to Flanders and other countries on the continent.

A royal mint was established in Berwick by 1153 and the eleventh and twelfth centuries saw the development of a cash economy. Prior to this, trade would have been mainly by barter. In 1153, David was succeeded by Malcolm IV, a boy of eleven years, and the first mention of a Berwick castle occurs in his reign. Not long after his accession, Malcolm was summoned by the first of the Plantagenet English kings, Henry II, and he was forced to return Northumbria to England.

Malcolm's successor, William the Lion, resented the loss of Northumbria and invaded England in 1174, and ravaged the English northern counties before falling back to Berwick 'to their lodgings', as a chronicler puts it. There they enjoyed the spoils of their raiding with 'much amusement'. With the advancing English armies near, William withdrew from Berwick which then suffered the full fury of the enemy. Berwick was burnt and the surrounding country wasted. Southern Scotland was subdued, for Berwick Castle as well as Jedburgh and Roxburgh castles were

These silver pennies were minted in Berwick (Vila Bervice) between 1250 and 1310. At this time, Berwick was prominent as a mint not only in the reign of Alexander III of Scotland, but also in the reign of Edward I of England. Alexander's mintmaster (or moneyer) was John (upper coins), the lower coins being Edward's with no moneyer named. The site of the mint would probably be the castle.

held by Henry's English soldiers, while Northumbria was definitely English again. William was subsequently captured at Alnwick, while on another war expedition into England. He was humiliated by being led on horseback in ritual procession into Northampton, his feet tied beneath his mount. He was thrown into a dungeon in Falaise, Normandy, and was forced to accept the King of England as his feudal overlord, and was subsequently released.

Berwick's castle, along with other castles in the south of Scotland, was eventually redeemed in 1189, after a large sum of money was paid to the new English King. This was Richard I, who spent all the royal revenues in financing his passion for fighting in the Crusades. The castle at Berwick by now had been strengthened. Originally, its defences would have been wooden, with strong stakes set together making a wall round the high ground, with the declivity behind (Castle Vale Park) and the steep drop in the ground to the west being strong natural defence features. These natural features would have been a decisive factor in siting the castle, as would the all-round outlook it afforded, overlooking a natural fording place through the River Tweed. The upgrading of the castle by Henry II probably saw stone walls replacing the wooden ones, and because the hill the castle was built on is a natural feature, the heavier stone would present no foundation difficulties. On an artificial hill or motte, stone could not readily replace wood due to possible slippage of the earth.

Across the river in Tweedmouth, some fifteen years after the castle of Berwick passed back into Scottish hands, King John of England began building a fort. While not on the same scale as the castle at Berwick, it nevertheless posed a threat, and William, who had by now ruled Scotland for thirty-nine years, objected, sent his forces over the river and razed it to the ground. It was again built and again it was demolished. Five uneasy years passed until a treaty was drawn up – John would give up tower-building and William would provide two of his daughters to be conveniently wedded to two sons of John – a neat solution! As the Scottish King's daughters came with a dowry

of 1,000 marks (£666 13s 4d) as part recompense for the slight done to John's prestige in having his forts destroyed, it was felt that honours were even.

At this time Berwick was the premier burgh in Scotland, its burgeoning trade dependent on a flourishing cloth industry and export of wool to Flanders. The close association Scotland had with Flanders through the Flemish settlement in Berwick is typified in a chronicle which describes how the King's messengers were to find boatmen at Berwick who would take them to Flanders. They were to ask the Counts of Flanders for assistance in future battles, and on the journey they would not sail down the coast of England where their enemies were, but presumably would strike eastwards into the North Sea before turning south for the Low Countries. This would appear to be a testament to the skill of the mariners of Berwick, who could set a course for the Continent without having to hug the coastline of England down to the English Channel. It is interesting that in Bruges to this day there is a street name 'Scottish Street', testifying to the close links forged by trade over the centuries.

In Berwick, foreign merchants, factors and shippers abounded. As well as being Scotland's largest town, Berwick would be akin to a foreign trading colony. In the Seagate (in the lower part of the town, probably near the present Shoregate) was the Red Hall, the headquarters for the Flemish merchants, and also the White Hall, the base of the German traders. The Red Hall may have derived its name from being built from imported Flemish red bricks, or perhaps from the red Flemish pantiles, which were known to have roofed many of the Berwick houses subsequently. The White Hall may just have been lime-washed.

Many foreign ships would make their voyages from the continent to dock at Berwick, for it is known that of the ships with Scottish cargoes wrecked on the English coast in the fourteenth

An engraving of a painting by J.M.W. Turner who visited Berwick in August 1831, staying at the King's Arms. A mill with an overshot water wheel is depicted on the left (in Tommy the Miller's field). The extensive walls and high towers are quite prominent, being almost twenty years before the coming of the railway destroyed most of the remains of the castle. Tweedmouth is shown with the water lapping the sides of the houses, and salmon fishermen are busy on both sides of the river.

Above the door of a merchant's house in Ghent in Flanders, is a realistic carving of a merchant ship of the type in use in the Middle Ages. At this time, large quantities of wool from the Border abbeys were shipped from Berwick to Ghent and other towns in the Low Countries.

century, more than half had come from Flanders.

Not only Berwick, but other Scottish burghs had a considerable number of foreigners resident in their towns. Many of Berwick's inhabitants spoke Flemish, and as the most prosperous Royal Burgh in Scotland with a population of just a few thousand, perhaps 15 per cent would be speaking a foreign tongue.

Between 1174 and 1292, Scotland and England were mostly at peace. Alexander II and Alexander III of Scotland between them ruled for seventy-two years. This time of peace allowed for settled villages in the area, with the surrounding land round the villages being divided into what was known as 'ploughgates', or areas that could be worked by one team of oxen each. At the bottom of the social ladder were the peasants, who owned nothing but paid by their labour or in kind for their occupation of land or homes. They ate simply when times were good, and when times were bad they went hungry. Wheat, peas, beans, cheese and some meat figured in their diet, and fish was usually available. For liquid nourishment, they had ale which would be brewed locally, and which had no hops in it. The bigger landowners and the religious houses would have imported wine. The ordinary folk were pressed into military service for the king when required, but anyone owning land had to keep at least one horse, which would be available for the king in times of war. Life at this time for those who toed the line would have been tolerable; for those who did not, the law provided the gallows.

A Flemish cog. This type of ship would have been very commonly seen in Berwick in the thirteenth and fourteenth centuries. It was one of the most important and capacious types of merchant ships, which would sail between Berwick and Flanders taking wool and hides and returning with cloth and other manufactured goods, including wine and beer.

An engraving of Norham Castle from the painting by J.M.W. Turner. It was said that Turner always doffed his hat on seeing Norham Castle for he said his painting of it had made his name.

An unfortunate blip in the otherwise peaceful period occurred in 1215, when Alexander II of Scotland besieged Norham Castle for forty days. Unsuccessful, he retired northwards and poor old Berwick once again took the reprisal. In January 1216, when King John was fifty years of age and in the last year of his life, he stormed Berwick and took the castle and the town, besides burning Roxburgh, Dunbar and Haddington to teach the 'fox cub' a lesson (Alexander II was only eighteen). John is described as the most vicious, short-sighted, tyrannical and unscrupulous of English monarchs, and he is shown at his worst in his behaviour in Berwick. He is said to have suspended men and women by their fingers and toes and caused them to be tortured inhumanly, and his soldiers were supposed to have been coached in this wickedness by several individuals brought with them specially to provide tuition. John even burnt the house he had slept in the previous night, no doubt in one of the fits of rage to which he was liable, when, it is said, he was capable of eating straws and small sticks.

The purpose of Alexander II's foray against Norham was chiefly to regain Northumberland, which he regarded as part of the lost territory which belonged rightly to Scotland. He was also giving support to the English barons, who eventually forced King John to sign the *Magna Carta*, which is today regarded as the foundation of democracy and the rule of law in this country. Eventually, Alexander gave up the idea of regaining Northumberland, and accepted a number of northern English estates in settlement of his claims. Alexander was excommunicated by the Pope, for allying himself with Louis of France, but the next year (1217) he received absolution at Tweedmouth, at the hands of the Archbishop of York and the Bishop of Durham, when they held a papal council there.

The seal of Alexander III of Scotland shows the young King on his throne (he was seven when he succeeded to the crown), and also as a fully armed warrior on his horse.

Henry III became King of England after the hated John, and subsequently Alexander II of Scotland married Henry's sister Joan. Alexander died in 1249 and his body was buried in Melrose Abbey. He was succeeded by his son, Alexander III, aged eight. Two years later, Alexander was married to his cousin Margaret, daughter of Henry III of England, and prospects looked bright for peace and stability between England and Scotland, the two royal families being thus linked so closely by marriage.

So it proved, and during Alexander III's reign Berwick's prosperity grew. Berwick was now referred to as 'the noble town of Berwick, belonging to the King of Scots'. The population no doubt increased, as its commercial importance grew, and Berwick was referred to as 'a second Alexandria, whose riches was the sea and the water was its walls'. A chronicler writes of merchant princes of Berwick, and how they were generous in their gifts to the Church, so much so that almost every abbey in Scotland had property in Berwick. In 1286 Berwick's customs revenue paid to the Scottish exchequer was equal to one quarter of the whole customs of England.

About this time Alexander III's wine bill to one wine merchant in the Bordeaux region of France, came to £2,000, a colossal amount in those days. But there was no problem with this and other debts, for the Berwick revenue was assigned to pay the creditors. This was the Golden Age of Berwick indeed, but the good times would not last much longer. The kings of Scotland over this prosperous period had visited and sojourned in Berwick frequently, and indeed the present-day streets of Palace Street, East and West, and especially Palace Green reminds us of a time when the king's royal dwelling might have been sited in this area. Probably courts were held and charters signed in the castle, and regal marriages and birthdays celebrated in great style. People would travel to Berwick for these occasions, for the roads were good and wheeled vehicles were in use at the time. Events which befell Berwick subsequently ensured that wheeled vehicles would rarely be seen for more than four centuries thereafter. Perhaps the good life was not conducive to religious sanctity in the thirteenth century, for it is noted that the Cistercians of Berwick were excommunicated by Papal decree, because of their 'riotous and refractory behaviour'.

The Golden Age for Scotland came to a sudden end with the King's death in 1286. Alexander III, anxious to be in Kinghorn with his French wife of only five months, disregarded advice to tarry overnight on the journey home, and instead pressed on in the dark. His horse stumbled, the King was thrown and he was killed. As the chronicler wrote:

Translation

'Quhen Alysander our Kyng was dede	When Alexander Our King was dead
That Scotland led in luve and le	That Scotland led in love and loyalty,
Awaye was sons of ale and brede	Away was sons of ale and bread
Of wyne and wax, of gaymn and gle;	Of wine and plenty of game and glee,
Our gold was changed into lede	Our gold was changed into lead
Cryst borne into virginite	Christ, born into virginity
Succour Scotland and remede	Succour Scotland and remedy
That stad is in perplexitye.'	That place is in perplexity.

CHAPTER 3
Warring Years

Once again, the future of Scotland was in the melting pot, and Berwick, like as not, would be in the furnace! Alexander's heir was his grandchild, Margaret, infant daughter of the King of Norway. Six guardians were appointed to govern Scotland until such time as Margaret (Maid of Norway) would arrive to ascend the throne – she was only three. At this time, the relationship between the nobility and royals of England and Scotland was intricate, for the kings of Scotland paid homage and fealty to the English king for their lands in England.

Edward I (known as Longshanks) had by now been King of England for eighteen years. He was approached by the six guardians for advice, and he proposed that his son should be betrothed to the infant Margaret which would result in a dynastic union between the two countries. A ship was sent to Norway for Margaret with a present for the little girl from Edward, consisting of sweets and raisins. Poor little Margaret died on the voyage to Scotland, possibly from terrible sea-sickness, for it was a stormy voyage.

Prior to the proposed marriage, legal arrangements between England and Scotland were made. This was in the form of a treaty and it was drawn up at the village of Birgham, 16 miles west of Berwick, on the north side of the River Tweed. The treaty was carefully drafted envisaging as it did two kingdoms linked by marriage, but ruled as separate entities. On the death of Margaret, Edward I considered the treaty (which would have made for a peaceful co-existence between the two nations) null and void.

Now there was a vacuum in the government of Scotland and claimants to the throne came rushing to fill the void. Guidance was sought from Edward I, and no doubt the Pope himself was holding a watching brief, for some years later he offered himself as an arbitrator. He was

The old cattle market is shown at the top of this photograph (c. 1909), and this was the site of the Dominican chapel where Edward I heard claims from contenders for the Scottish throne. Cyclists' battalions of soldiers were a feature of the First World War, some fighting in Russia against the Bolsheviks at Archangel in 1919.

Berwick railway station (c. 1899) illustrates the determined effort the North British Railway company made to emulate the castle it had destroyed when bringing the railway to Berwick in 1846.

told by the English Parliament to mind his own business, and subsequently, in the Declaration of Arbroath, the Scottish Parliament asserted its independence, and warned the Pope against favouring the English.

But to return to the local scene: in the summer of 1291, momentous happenings were taking place at Norham, seven miles from Berwick. Meetings were held at which Edward I presided, first on the open plain on the Haugh opposite Norham Castle, then in Norham church, and finally in Norham Castle. Claims were heard by Edward from the various rivals to the throne over a period of two months. In the middle of August the hearings were moved to the Dominican chapel in Berwick. This was sited at the top of Castlegate on the north side, where there is now a car-wash, lock-ups and a tattoo parlour. No decision was reached and the hearings were postponed for a year. In June and July 1292, more meetings were held in the chapel, but no decision was taken and it was further postponed to the autumn. Could this perhaps indicate that Edward was enjoying his summer holiday in Berwick too much, and preferred to leave thorny decisions until the days shortened? More likely, Edward was turning the screw ever tighter over the lengthy proceedings, upping his demands for recognition of his overlordship of Scotland. At any rate, the momentous decision was made in the great hall of Berwick Castle on 17 November 1292. John Balliol was the winner by a short hair and the elderly Robert Bruce the loser. Robert died in 1295 at the age of eighty-five, not knowing his grandson, then aged twenty-one, would become King Robert the Bruce of Scotland 'brave in heart and hand'.

Two days later, Edward of England gave sasine (or possession) of Scotland to Balliol, along with the castle of Berwick. At one time, this was done by the symbolic handing over of a piece of turf and a stone, but however the handing over of title was done, Edward broke the old seal of Scotland into four parts and placed them in the Treasury. This was a measure of Edward's power, and was indicative of his sovereignty over Scotland.

Balliol became known as Toom Tabard, or empty jacket, ostensibly because he was a vassal of Edward, and had no real power. Friction between the rulers began almost immediately, and one of the causes involved a legal appeal made by the widow of a Berwick goldsmith, William Aurifaber. Marjory the widow had four children to support, and the dowry which her late husband had contracted to give her was being held illegally, by one Roger Bartholomew (who appears in the list of burgesses who swore loyalty to Edward in 1291). The Mayor of Berwick, Philip Rydale, owed William the goldsmith thirteen sacks of wool, and this was ordered to be handed over in lieu of the dowry. This award was made by the Scottish court, but was overturned on appeal to the English court, which Edward averred was the higher authority. Thus was Edward's power over Balliol illustrated.

Edward was now at war with France. Known as Edward Longshanks, because of his big frame, he was a powerful man, and though subsequently given the epithet Hammer of the Scots, he hammered others as well, including the Jews whom he banished from the kingdom. Consequently, he was less than pleased when he discovered Balliol had allied himself with France, for he expected the Scottish armies to help him. Wales was also in revolt, for they did not see why they should support Edward's armies in his conquest and claims in France.

Balliol, to help his French ally, summoned his armies to march against England, the assembly point for his invasion force to be at Caddonlea, a mile out of Galashiels. Balliol attacked Carlisle, and in return Edward assaulted Scotland's jewel, Berwick – for it was the premier port and wool centre of Scotland. Edward's army was massive by any standard. One account writes of 5,000 horsemen and 30,000 foot soldiers, and even if this number was exaggerated, they did wreak awful havoc. In addition, it is stated that a fleet of 100 vessels would be ready to co-operate with the land army. Edward did not assault Berwick directly from the south, but forded the Tweed near Coldstream, where he camped overnight. After another night's camp at Hutton, he arrived with the bulk of his army on 30 March 1296 at Nunslees, one mile north east of Berwick (the area between High Letham and the junction of the Duns road with the bypass). The town of Berwick was prepared for an assault, and in their ignorance the citizens were confident of victory. Fife soldiers garrisoned the town, and the castle was manned and commanded by a doughty fighter named William Douglas. The townspeople were supposed to have shouted insults and taunted Edward, which in retrospect was foolish in the extreme, for he had a violent and unstable temper. An old French chronicle records the insults thus:

'What wende the Kyng Edward,
For his lange shanks,
For to wynne Berewyke
All our unthankes
Go Pike it him
And when he have it won
Go Dike it him.'

Omens of disaster had been observed before Edward's onslaught, according to the *Lanercost Chronicle* (1296). Before Christmas 1295, some Berwick children who were hastening to school just after dawn, saw Christ on the cross beyond the castle, his face covered with blood and looking towards the town. Another dread sign was a great ball of fire coming from the south, which spread over Berwick as if consuming everything. It then went north before disappearing in the sky having destroyed everything in its path, which of course was the route that Edward

over

Herring boats beating up the estuary in 1900 in much the same way as Edward I's naval vessels did when launching the attack on the town in 1296.

took after the sack of Berwick. No matter what the portents of disaster foretold, the die was now cast. The navy struck first, the vessels coming up the estuary with the tide, but they were driven back by fire attacks, men, women and children helping to make faggots with which to set the ships alight. Edward, seeing the defenders were fully occupied by the waterside, breached the defences to the north of the town. Edward's steed had the name Bayard (after a horse of remarkable swiftness which had belonged to one of the knights of Charlemagne). On this he leaped over a stockade and ditch and his armies poured into the town. The Flemish community in their headquarters the Red Hall offered the greatest resistance, all perishing in the fire which consumed the building. Some citizens of Berwick took refuge in the churches, but to no avail, for they were slaughtered without mercy. Thousands were killed and every building was sacked, and it is said that with the slaughter and desecration of Berwick, the seeds were sown in Scotland for a hatred of the English which was to last for centuries. The total number of citizens killed is impossible to calculate, but it was written that the streets ran with blood and the mill wheels were being turned by the quantity of blood flowing through the millstreams. The castle had capitulated without a fight even though it was garrisoned by 200 men. These men were allowed to leave with their arms, and their estates were not forfeited, after they promised Edward they would never take up arms against the Kingdom of England. William Douglas, the captain, was taken prisoner, so if he thought he would gain favour with the King by his surrender, he obviously made a miscalculation.

It is strange that the Flemish merchants made such a determined stand, for previously they had recognized Edward as their overlord, and it might be thought that they had every reason to negotiate or surrender. It might suggest that, aware of Edward's unstable temper (for many would have met him), and his reputation for vindictiveness, that consequently they thought they had nothing to lose by making a spirited defence.

Edward, victorious, stayed in the castle for almost a month, during which time he gave orders for the strengthening of Berwick's defences. Edward is supposed to have laboured in the work himself, but this could be apocryphal. A huge foss (trench) was dug between the northern side of the castle and the sea, running through the Magdalene fields (the Golf Course), and finishing somewhere near where Leith the tent maker's premises now are, on Pier

Photographed in the 1960s, this aerial view shows the layout of the streets. In particular, the line of Hide Hill on the right continuing up Church Street to Wallace Green suggests this might have been the main route to the north from the ford which came across the river somewhere near the Shoregate. This was long before the Elizabethan walls were built in the sixteenth century, which cut off the continuation through to Low Greens and Scotland.

Road. It would be walled, for accounts of the expense of making a wall to the Snook (near Windmill Bastion on the Elizabethan Walls) do exist. The depression in the ground known today as Spade's Mire may be part of this defensive ditch. A wall was built, between the castle and the river, which still stands. Known as the White Wall, it is stepped and has loops for the firing of arrows or bolts by defenders. It would have been covered and provided a passage down to a water tower on the river, which was another defensive feature.

over

Part of Edward I's wall above Castle Vale park (entrance from Station Yard) dating from the thirteenth or fourteenth century.

Now, it would appear, Berwick was being rebuilt, but it was as an English garrison town. The English army under the Earl of Surrey (Balliol's brother-in-law) had in their number Robert Bruce and his adherents, another indication of how the Scots were deeply divided. They marched on Dunbar, where they were greeted with taunts, the Scots shouting 'Come hither, ye long tailed hounds, and we will cut off your tails for you!' A slaughter of the Scots ensued and Dunbar castle was taken. Thereafter, the main castles of Scotland fell, King John Balliol was taken prisoner and Scotland was completely under Edward's domination.

Edward put a final stamp on his victory, by holding a parliament in Berwick on 28 August 1296. A record was made of the Scottish nobility and gentry subscribing allegiance to Edward at this time. This list, known as the *Ragman Roll*, recorded over 1,500 names, but it had nothing to do with rags, for it derived its name from one Ragimunde, who had earlier drawn up a similar list. At any rate, with their oaths of fealty, the signatories to the list ensured that Scotland was more or less a colony of England.

The ancient Crowning Stone of Scone had been brought to Berwick by Edward, who had it sent to London along with the Scottish regalia. Edward said dismissively of Balliol, who was now a prisoner in London, 'A man does good business when he rids himself of a turd'. Edward set up a government to rule Scotland, and established an exchequer in Berwick to receive the revenues from Scotland. Edward believed that Berwick could be improved if the Scots residents were displaced and their houses given to English settlers.

It may be thought today that the position of planning officer for Berwick is a new innovation, but in fact Berwick had its first planning officer 700 years ago in the shape of Edward I. He drew up a programme of meetings, at which learned men from various English towns were to advise on the planning of a new town (Berwick) 'to the most profit of the King and of the merchants'. Three meetings were held of this town planning committee, but nothing was ever done – things have not changed! Attention was, however, given to the defensive needs of Berwick over the next five years, for it was hard to keep the lid on the

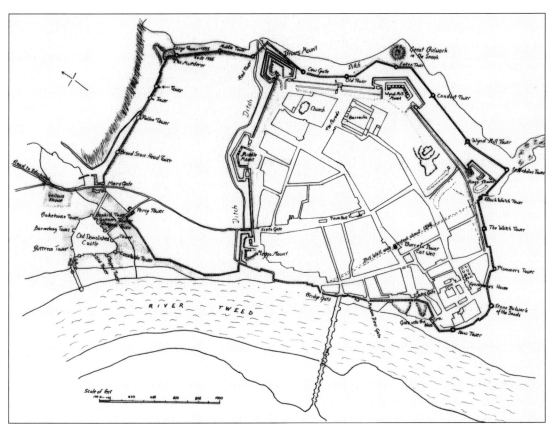

The line of both the Edwardian and Elizabethan walls can be seen on this plan of 1745, as well as the projected Cat Well wall cutting off the lower part of the town.

bubbling pot which was Scotland. The levies imposed on Scotland, which were paid to the exchequer in Berwick, began to dry up, and it appeared that Edward would have to subsidize his operations in Scotland rather than receive revenue from his northern domain.

The Earl of Surrey had been appointed by Edward as his senior overseer of Scotland, both in a military sense and also civil, for he had to administer justice and make decisions regarding religious orders. He lacked enthusiasm for his office, did not like the weather in this area, and even attempted to pass the burden to someone else. The Berwick government was being challenged more and more, culminating in a Scottish rising in 1297, led by a guerrilla chief, William Wallace. John de Warenne (the Earl of Surrey) bestirred himself and with a formidable army of cavalry, archers and foot soldiers, marched north to meet Wallace at Stirling. The King's Treasurer in Berwick rode with him, one Hugh de Cressingham. Cressingham was a hated man in Scotland, for as Treasurer, he had extorted money from the Scots. He was even disliked by the English and was described as voluptuous, selfish, proud, ignorant and opinionated. He was also mean, and had held back the building of the stone walls round Berwick, ordered by Edward, on account of the expense. The English nobles despised him as a bastard, and no doubt the troops also referred to him thus, for he withheld their pay unjustly! The English army was greatly

over

Plan of 1570 showing the centre of the town with what is thought to be the Tollbooth or Town Hall adjacent to the Town Cross. The gardens and yards behind the houses have not been built on and the pattern of the streets shown here is probably the same as it was in Edward I's time.

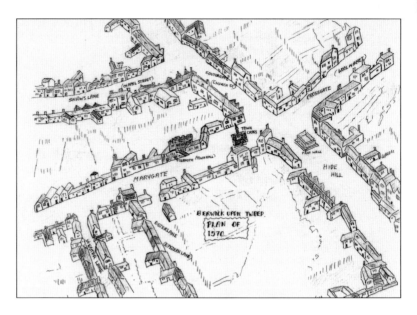

superior in numbers to Wallace's and was well seasoned in war. The Scottish army had built a confidence from successful guerrilla tactics under Wallace's leadership, but the odds were stacked against them. Surrey sent two friars to offer Wallace terms of surrender – Wallace replied, 'Tell your people that we have not come here to gain peace, but are prepared for battle, to avenge and deliver our country.' Wallace's position was on an upward slope overlooking Stirling Bridge, and Surrey was hesitant in ordering his troops to advance. Cressingham urged him on, saying, 'There is no use in drawing out this business any longer, and wasting our King's revenues for nothing.' Another example of his meanness, perhaps.

Wallace held back his army until he judged the numbers of the English who had crossed the bridge could be dealt with, and with savage flanking attacks the outcome was disaster for Surrey who promptly took the road for Berwick. He is supposed to have fled with such haste on his horse, that when it was put into its stable in a friary in Berwick, it promptly expired – it literally had been ridden to death. The treasurer of the Berwick government was not so lucky. Cressingham had been killed in the battle, and it was reported his body was skinned, with pieces taken as souvenirs, and one long piece made into a baldrick (or sword belt) for Wallace.

Edward was in Flanders fighting against the French for control of his French possessions in Gascony. Making a peace treaty with the French, he returned to take charge of the situation. Meantime, the Scots took Berwick without much trouble, for the inhabitants had fled, emulating Surrey's flight from Stirling. The castle, however, being well defended, remained as part of Edward's possessions. It must have been an impressive fortress with a central tower, a great hall, forge, chapel, bake house, and all the other usual chambers associated with a self-contained community.

William Douglas, who had been captain of Berwick Castle when the garrison surrendered to Edward's men in 1296, had been released from prison. After swearing fealty to Edward, he regained his liberty and estate, but when Wallace took on the mantle of leadership (supporting the cause of Balliol) Douglas was one of the first persons of eminence to support

Towers and curtain-walls
1 Hoardings   2 Base of tower   3 Crenelle   4 Merlon
5 Arrow slit or lancet   6 Curtain-walls

Berwick Castle in the thirteenth century would not have been unlike this representation. The crenelles are the cuts in the top of the walls, the merlons being the intervening parts. These openings allowed the archers to shoot at their enemies.

The longbow gave the English infantry a superiority over all other arms for over 100 years in the thirteenth and fourteenth centuries. It was accurate, with a low trajectory and long range. It was also very powerful and speedy in use, the effective range being 250 yards.

him. He was recaptured by the English and again he was placed in irons and incarcerated in the castle of which he had been captain.

Another who could change sides was Henry de Haliburton, who had taken Berwick after the battle of Stirling Bridge, despite having rendered homage to Edward in 1296. Henry accompanied Wallace on his raiding in the north of England, and subsequently was leader of the Scots who were besieging Berwick Castle which had held out for three months. Henry, a Scottish knight, was a Borderer, his lands being in Berwickshire, and it is interesting that Wallace's men must have been drawn mainly from the southern part of Scotland, for very few of them came from north of the River Tay. This was probably because Wallace was looked down on by many of the Earls and Nobles (with their estates in the north), for Wallace by their thinking was not of royal blood. Wallace's forces were made up of the peasants, the farmers, the small lairds and their sons, also the craftsmen burgesses. A great part of his army must have been drawn from the wasted lands of the Borders, for the people had been continually forced to flee from their homes, sometimes starving, which would fuel their white-hot resentment of the English.

A MEDIEVAL LONG-BOW MAN

over

At the beginning of 1298, Berwick was again taken by the English, the Scottish forces having left when hearing of the advancing enemy. In May 1298, the English army in Berwick was awaiting the arrival of Edward from Flanders, for he was going to lead them against Wallace personally. The castle was given into the custody of the Earl of Dunbar, and 500 men-at-arms from Gascony in France were garrisoning Berwick. The King was in debt, for apart from his forays in Flanders, the upkeep of Berwick was making inroads in his finances. His insatiable need to subdue the Scots was not to be denied, and borrowing money on the strength of customs revenues (including Berwick's), he prepared to do battle. Supplies were loaded into a ship in Berwick, for the provisioning of Maiden Castle (Edinburgh) and Stirling.

Wallace was decisively beaten at the Battle of Falkirk, despite various mishaps which befell Edward and his army before the fray. The Welsh allies of Edward got drunk, and threatened to desert him; provisions for the army had not come up the Forth by ship as arranged, and finally Edward was kicked by his horse and sustained two broken ribs. Despite all this, the English archers, using their long-bows, broke the Scottish schiltrons (semi-circular or hedgehog-like formations of spearmen, interspersed with archers), and Edward could now subdue the rest of Scotland, taking the castles of Stirling, Cupar and Ayr, and laying waste Perth and St Andrews.

Jedburgh was still in the hands of the Scots, and Edward ordered coal, iron, and steel to be sent from Berwick for the siege engines, which would be used against Jedburgh castle, which submitted. Edward now placed large garrisons in all the southern castles. In Berwick, sixty men-at-arms and 1,000 foot soldiers were billeted, and orders were given that no one in the town of Berwick was to venture out against the enemy, unless accompanied by half the garrison, i.e. thirty men-at-arms and 500 foot soldiers. This would imply that despite the defeat at Falkirk, the Scots were still warring, and the danger from the north was still very real.

Edward indented provisions from various parts of his kingdom, all to be sent to Berwick where a ship was always to be ready to take supplies to Edinburgh, or wherever required. He had his mind set on another invasion in 1299, and indeed he spent the winter of 1298/99 in Berwick awaiting favourable conditions. However, a truce with Scotland was arranged, and this held for a few years. All was not well in Berwick, however, for the garrison was in a state of mutiny, not having been paid. The garrison was largely made up of Gascon mercenaries from the south-west of France and threats were made that throats would be cut if payment was not forthcoming. A few days later the money arrived, and after a 'pay-day', order was restored, but this must have worried Edward, for Berwick was the mainspring of his administration mechanism for Scotland.

By 1305, Edward had conducted four more annual forays into Scotland, the inhabitants of Berwick, willingly or otherwise, helping to provision his campaigns. Berwick continued to be storehouse and victualling centre for the castles of Roxburgh and Jedburgh. Edward, by royal right of purveyance (requisition) demanded large quantities of wheat, oats, malt and pulses to be sent to Berwick from various counties in the south. He did not always get the quantities he wanted, sometimes because of genuine scarcity, other times because of resentment engendered by the rapacious demands the King was making to carry on the war.

In 1301 Edward was in Berwick in July with a huge force of 7,000 foot soldiers and hundreds of archers. Another force of over 2,000 assembled in the west. Some eighty-one ships were summoned to assemble at Berwick, including twelve large ships from the Cinque Ports – a

Though this engraving was produced in 1745, this scene with its press of ships might not be dissimilar to that of 1301, when Edward I was assembling his forces in Berwick for yet another foray into Scotland.

huge fleet. The campaign was inconclusive, and the strain on the Royal exchequer was now becoming acute.

The next year (1302) saw the burgesses of Berwick asserting themselves, by pointing out to the King that his proposal to grant forty acres 'lying between the town and its fosses to an interloper' was injurious to them. The 'interloper' was the King's sergeant in Berwick, but interestingly most of the burgesses were newcomers also, or 'inti-loupers' as the local term has it. In the judgement, Edward granted a new charter of privileges, but of course it was a charter given under English favour whereas the previous charter was given by a Scottish king's favour.

In 1303 supplies were again being indented to be sent to Berwick before the end of May, and the people who were being taxed to pay for the supplies were undoubtedly rebellious. One hundred ships were ordered north, half to come to Berwick and the other half to proceed to Ayr on the west coast. In the first days of this year, Sir John Seagrave, captain of Northumberland with his company at Berwick, could not prevent the loss of a newly constructed fortress at Selkirk. The next month, he and his men were ambushed near Roslin. Edward's army, moving north, started to experience problems due to the lack of money being sent to him to pay his army and even his royal cooks.

Grain indented in Somerset and Dorset was urgently needed in Berwick to feed the army and the citizens, so ships and crews were commandeered to bring the supplies. A pontoon bridge stored in Berwick along with six engines of war and supplies of victuals were shipped to Edward who by now was trying to recapture Stirling Castle, which he did in 1304. Effectively this was the successful conclusion which Edward wanted, and the Scottish leaders in submission were made responsible for handing over William Wallace.

over

Wallace had been continuing resistance, and for the previous four years had been making guerrilla attacks on the English forces. He was reported at times in the Forest of Selkirk (Ettrick Forest), where the denseness of the trees and thickets gave cover. In 1301 he gained an ally in the person of Sir Simon Fraser, Edward's keeper of Ettrick Forest. Fraser, a Scotsman, had been captured by Edward's forces at the battle of Dunbar. Thereafter, he joined the opposite side and fought in Flanders for Edward. There, he covered himself with glory, and was rewarded by the return of his estate and appointed as keeper of the Forest.

His loyalties seem to have always been with the Scots, however; indeed, he may all along have been acting as an agent for them. In 1301, he suddenly left Wark Castle on the Tweed, taking another knight's armour and horse and joining Wallace. The king for whom they were fighting (John Balliol) was in France, and he was a broken reed. He was not likely to return, and support for Wallace was waning. Despite some overtures on behalf of Wallace for a settlement, Edward would accept nothing but unconditional surrender. Edward's hatred of Wallace seemed to warp his judgement, for while he would negotiate with the Scottish nobles, Wallace was expressly excluded from any bargaining or clemency. It may be that he regarded Wallace's ideas of freedom and liberty for the individual as a contagion, which could spread to his own kingdom, so he was branded a traitor and liable to a traitor's death.

Wallace was captured on 3 August 1305, betrayed, it is said, by Sir John Menteith. Menteith, like Sir Simon Fraser, had fought against the English at the Battle of Dunbar, and subsequently fought for Edward in Flanders, as an alternative to being kept in prison. He then rejoined the Scots for five years, but finally rejoined Edward who rewarded him by giving him the custody of Dumbarton castle. He was later given a large sum of money for his services in Wallace's capture. Wallace was taken to London on 22 August 1305, a Sunday. The next day, he was taken on horseback to Westminster for his trial. Sir John de Segrave commanded the escort. Segrave, former keeper of Berwick castle and captain of Northumberland, was also one of the judges at Wallace's trial. Wallace was found guilty of treason, but as he had never sworn allegiance to Edward he answered that he had never been a traitor. At Smithfield he died an agonizing death. He had been dragged on a hurdle through the streets of London to a specially constructed high gallows. An English chronicler recorded: 'He was hung in a noose, and afterwards let down half living; next his genitals were cut off and his bowels torn out and burnt in a fire; then and not till then, his head was cut off and his trunk cut into four pieces.' The head was stuck on a spear and fixed upon London Bridge. Sir John de Segrave of Berwick was in charge of the distribution of the quarters of the body and the right leg was sent to Berwick, other parts going to Stirling, Perth and Newcastle. Not long after, the head of his friend Sir Simon Fraser joined that of Wallace, 'in the sight of all who passed by land or water' and this gory display was 'for terror and rebuke to all who should pass by and behold them'.

Berwick by this time was being anglicized, for most of the burgesses were English who had been re-settled there as part of Edward's plan. Nonetheless, the fact that one of Wallace's limbs was on display there as a warning that no-one should step out of line, suggests that anti-English feeling still existed there. It has been suggested that Wallace Green in Berwick was where the grisly remains of the Scottish patriot were hung; alternatively that he once had his encampment there, or had entered Berwick at that point. Whatever the truth, there is little doubt that Wallace deserves to be remembered in Berwick, for he lit a flame of democracy, not just for Scotland, but for all the other parts of what we now call the British Isles, for he demonstrated by his actions that the freedom of a country is more important than the rights of a king.

Another patriot whose name lives on in a Berwick street was Bruce, once Wallace's comrade, and grandson of Robert Bruce who was denied the Scottish throne in 1292 by Edward's decision in Berwick.

Edward I was an old man when he died in 1307 aged sixty-eight, but he never gave up on his 'hammering' of the Scots. He was enraged when he learned that Robert Bruce was now King Robert of Scotland. Robert had taken himself to Scone, the ancient Scottish crowning place, and had been crowned by the Countess of Buchan, with William Lamberton, Bishop of St Andrews in attendance. It was her brother's right to crown the kings of Scotland but he did not dare to do so. For her temerity, Edward had her imprisoned in the castle at Berwick in one of the towers, and likewise Bruce's sister was imprisoned in Roxburgh castle. Bruce's brother along with his compatriots were sent to Berwick to be tried, where they were hung, drawn and quartered. Bruce was now on the run, and Edward, while dying, muttered imprecations against Scotland, ordering that his body be boiled and his bones carried in a bag at the head of his army until Scotland was crushed. So now it was Edward II *versus* Robert the Bruce, and yet again Berwick was destined to be the punch-bag!

Edward II was not the man his father was, but he had given his vow to his father that he would continue the fight to completely subjugate Scotland. In 1308 he ordered twenty ships to be ready to defend the east coast of England and especially the town of Berwick. Repeating his father's never-ending demands for provisions to be sent to the main base and storehouse of Berwick, wine was sent – 2,000 hogsheads (equivalent to 750,000 bottles of wine!), twenty barrels of honey and the usual wheat, oats, corn, barley etc., as well as feathered arrows of copper for the giant crossbows. Between forays into Scotland he passed at least one winter with his Queen in Berwick, where no doubt in the comfort of his castle, he could polish off any of the unused wine.

If the royal stomachs were upset, then the King and his Queen Isabella could turn to their resident apothecary in Berwick, one Odin. Apothecaries travelled with the royal entourage, and had done so since early medieval times. Their duties included the preparing of ointments and medicine as well as spicing the royal wine and embalming any royal corpses. Their equipment must have been quite formidable, for there is an account showing the money paid to Odin for the carriage of his coffers (containing his spices and medicines) from Berwick to Durham in the year 1311/12. One cartload was charged at 8d a day for five days, making a total of 3s 4d.

So life continued until in response to the raiding and wasting by Robert the Bruce who was attracting more adherents to his cause, Edward was pushed into action. The King was unpopular with the ruling barons of England, due to his rapacious demands for war funds, and singular lack of success against Scotland. Also, the King's favourite, Piers Gaveston, attracted the nobles' hatred because of his lifestyle. In older accounts of his character Piers is described as courageous, but also thriftless, witty and gay, and the last adjective can be ascribed to him in the modern sense as well. Edward II's 'gentle lord' Gaveston was beheaded by the barons, prompting in Edward a 'burst of grief'.

over

An artist's impression of Robert the Bruce as he was in 1306, taken from an old engraving.

So now an invasion of Scotland began in earnest in 1310, but to no avail, and a similar fate befell Edward's efforts in 1311 despite calling up 600 infantry from Northumberland without Parliament's permission. Recalled to face Parliament, Edward left Berwick in July, and Robert the Bruce immediately stepped up his activities, raiding and burning in the north of England and taking great quantities of booty. Growing bolder with more successes, Robert tried to take Berwick towards the end of the year 1312. Ingenious rope ladders were affixed to the walls of the castle with grappling irons in the dead of night, but the attempt failed when a dog gave the alarm by barking furiously.

The fatal year for Edward, 1314, began auspiciously with the mustering of a large army at Berwick. While the demands for troops made by the King were great by any account, it is quite possible that only half the numbers asked for did actually materialize. However, it is fairly evident that it was an impressive army, for 10,000 troops were ordered from the northern counties, and 10,000 from the south, in addition to masons, carpenters and smiths required for the building of engines of war. All these were to be ready for 19 May at Berwick, where the accumulation of victuals was going on apace. Space was at a premium in the town, and although some of the troops were lodged in Berwick in dwellings where the burgesses had been ejected, the majority were in tents

A mangonel – a military siege engine. The lever (1) is drawn down to the ground by the winch (2). When released, it flies up owing to the effect of the counter-weight (3). The sling on its tip holding the heavy missiles is propelled, projecting them to the target.

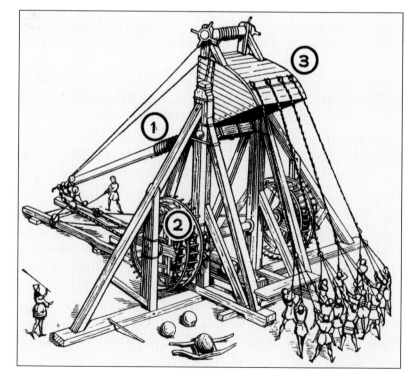

and pavilions (marquees) in the fields outwith the town. Huge trains of wagons carried the supplies; wagons with four horses (corectus) and wagons pulled by eight oxen (carras) stretched for miles. All roads led to Berwick, and when Edward saw his massive army, 'He wes rycht joyfull in his thocht', as the chronicler Barbour has written. Time was running out for Edward II, for the castles of Roxburgh and Edinburgh had fallen to Robert the Bruce.

Edward's allies in Scotland (for Robert had enemies who wanted power for themselves) were getting restive at Edward's lack of success. Stirling Castle was still in English hands, but Bruce had shown great ingenuity in capturing other castles. At Linlithgow, soldiers were smuggled into the castle under a load of hay and the cart used to jam the gates. Stirling therefore was the obvious objective for Edward, and Robert was prepared for him. Robert's army was mainly of peasant infantry and they had only light armour (which did not cover the body), axes, spears and shields. They formed a solid phalanx against the mounted English nobles, and had a well-chosen site. Before the battle, an English knight, Sir Henry de Bohun, was unlucky enough to encounter King Robert, who promptly split his head open with his axe with so much force that the haft was shattered. King Robert was later to lament the loss of his favourite axe! The outcome of the Battle of Bannockburn was a victory for Robert but not a victory which would ensure a permanent settlement, for within twenty years Scotland would be overrun again. Bruce had gambled on a direct engagement with the English, and it paid off handsomely in terms of the numerically superior English force being routed. The final blow to the English morale was when they thought Scottish reinforcements had arrived. In fact they were the *hoi polloi* – the carters and labourers for the army – who were moving in for the rich pickings to be taken from the dead and dying. Edward II was persuaded to leave the battlefield, and following the royal standard the English army retreated. Edward and his retinue sought refuge in Stirling castle, but were refused succour even though the castle was in English hands – the governor had promised to surrender the castle if not relieved that day. Some 30,000 English lay dead or dying, many having been drowned in the Bannock Burn as they retreated, others succumbing in the marshy ground.

Edward continued to Dunbar, having been hotly pursued from Stirling, a distance of 65 miles. It is said that he and his retinue only managed to escape, because the Scots were initially too concerned about looting the possessions of the slain. A ship was boarded at Dunbar and King Edward sailed south to Berwick in utter humiliation. He left for the south in September 1314, leaving Berwick and all the north of England under the jurisdiction of a captain, Adomarus de Valentia. Berwick was still 'a strong and well-walled town', and Edward took great concern to provision it and ensure its prosperity by allowing the burgesses to trade freely with anyone except the Scots. Ships came from London, Hull and other ports, with vast quantities of wheat, oats, barley and peas, all to be stored in case of attack, when the English armies would be required to rush to the defence. Two Berwick ships, named *Mariole* and *La Godyere*, assisted in the shipping of provisions, while Thomas of Chesewyk, servant of Walter of Gosewyk, was given safe conduct to guide a ship to Berwick, also laden with provisions.

The threat to Berwick was real enough, for in January 1316, on a bright, moonlit night, Bruce made a serious attack by land and sea. He obviously had received good intelligence reports, for his main thrust was between the Bridge House and the castle, 'where the walls were not yet built'. King Robert's navy must have been in the estuary, and rather like

over

This section of the walls near the Nessgate is medieval, the remaining bottom part of the semi-circular Black Watch tower being a striking feature which at its full height would have been even more impressive.

Dewar's Lane off Bridge Street has this huge leaning eighteenth-century granary, shown here when horses and carts were the means of transportation.

commandos in the Second World War, his 'marines' transferred into small skiffs to move upriver. They were spotted, the attempt failed, and Bruce's trusted lieutenant, Sir James Douglas, narrowly escaped in one of the skiffs.

Sir James Douglas, who was in charge of the marches of the Border, continued raiding in the north of England, becoming feared as no other, for his fighting prowess was legion. His base in Ettrick Forest allowed him to follow the precedent of Sir William Wallace who pioneered the idea of guerrilla attacks. A contradiction now appears in the records, for one account says that the garrison of Berwick was mostly composed of Gascons (mercenaries from south of Bordeaux in France) who, because they were starving, and without permission of the warden of Berwick, made a foray in the direction of Melrose to raid for cattle. This contrasts with the account of the victuals stored in Berwick, but perhaps the Gascons were denied access to the reserve stores, or more probably, poor harvests and continued raids by Bruce's men had reduced the victuals. At any rate the Gascons were caught by Sir James Douglas, and their booty was taken and many were killed. It would appear at this time that money was being paid by the burgesses of Bamburgh, also by such places as Norham and Islandshire to secure protection from raids. The area would have been depopulated to an extent, and without adequate husbandry, cattle would be diseased and crops lost. The terror of Sir James Douglas or the Black Douglas, as he was known, spread far and wide, and a citizen of London was sent to jail for a week for spreading false rumours that Douglas had invaded England, thereby causing 'fear and trembling of the people'. Even last century in the Borders, it was known that mothers would comfort their children by saying, 'Hush ye, hush ye, dinna fret ye – the Black Douglas will nae get ye'.

In the spring of 1316, things were chaotic in Berwick. Although the castle was in good order, having improved defences in the form of sally-ports, a bridge over the chasm, and good gates, and with the town's defences also strengthened, nevertheless men of the garrison were deserting. Lack of pay was one reason, and without pay the men could not buy victuals which in any case were in short supply. As in the two world wars of the twentieth century when cooks were known to purloin the best food and sell it for their own profit, so it was in Berwick. The cost of defending Edward's possessions was draining his exchequer, yet still did not provide protection for his subjects in the north, which by now was in a state of anarchy. Even some of Edward's own constables were acting as local warlords, and exacting money and goods from their own communities. The Earl of Pembroke with men-at-arms was hired to take pressure off the north, and after skirmishes he was defeated by a Scottish force at Longridge, just outside Berwick.

Supplies were being denied to Berwick by the activities of King Robert's ships which were in effect blockading the town. Flemish privateers were assisting in the blockade and Berwick was effectively under siege and becoming desperate. The warden of

The Sallyport is a passage through the walls allowing for a quick attack by defenders on attackers.

Cow Port, the only original gate in the Elizabethan Walls. It had a portcullis and a drawbridge over the moat.

Berwick was accused of being unjust to the population which was largely Scottish, and the situation was ripe for treasonable activities. That is to say, treasonable from the point of view of Edward, but not perhaps from the point of view of one Peter Spalding who was married to a cousin of Sir Robert Keith, Marshall of Scotland. Some accounts say he was given a large sum of money and land for his help in allowing the Scots entry to the town, but this may have been said to blacken his character subsequently. Some time about 1 April, the Scots scaled the walls near Cow Gate, perhaps when Spalding was keeping watch. Lying low until daybreak, the Scots spread out through the town, fighting any who resisted, and plundering as they went. The garrison in the castle rushed to the defence of Berwick but were driven back, and after six days of siege the castle was also taken.

Soon after the successful storming and taking of Berwick, King Robert came with his retinue, no doubt to congratulate his generals and survey his prize, for prize it undoubtedly was. After twenty years or more of trading under favourable English privileges, and despite its latter day privations, there would have been riches to be found in Berwick. Bruce, if he had followed his usual custom, would have razed the castle to the ground, so that it would be no asset to a future invader. Robert instead gave orders for the heightening of the walls, for he knew retaliation was sure to follow.

Edward II blamed the Mayor and Burgesses for a lack of resolve in defending the town, which they were obliged to do under the terms of a contract whereby they received the equivalent of £4,000 yearly. He resolved on immediate action and his navy, numbering over seventy ships, started its operations. The sailors in charge of the Cinque Ports fleet blockaded the estuary, and kept watch on the other entries and exits to the town. Edward II's troops numbered over 8,000, which included cavalry, archers and hobelars, who were men mounted on small horses. It would appear that trenches were dug by Edward's men, and these could only be for defensive purposes against Scots attacking from the landward area. The population of Berwick would have been swollen by people from the Borders, for King Robert had broadcast that settlers in Berwick would either get a built-on plot, or a plot and money – this did not apply to any from south of the Tweed! In addition Robert expelled any families who had collaborated with Edward, so that the citizens had every reason to rally to the defence of Berwick, for it was their own town, and Robert was their King. In the town were archers, spearmen and crossbowmen, also a secret weapon in the figure of John Crabbe, a Fleming. He was a skilled engineer who made cranes and engines of war, all designed to propel huge missiles against the enemy. Intriguingly, he could make 'Greek fire', which could strike terror in the hearts of an enemy force. It could well have had a similar effect on its victims to the flame throwers used in the Second World War, for it could be blown from tubes. It could burn on water, and even stone and iron could not resist it, being only extinguished by sand, vinegar or urine. Its components are a mystery though it is thought to have been based on naphtha, but the formula has been lost – perhaps fortunately.

Before Edward's first attempt to take Berwick some psychological warfare was employed on his behalf. Trumpets sounded, much merriment ensued, and his men enjoyed music and pleasure, all designed to show the contempt they had for the Scots. The Scots retaliated with coarse oaths and obscene gestures, and this tragi-comical scene may have been very similar to some of the antics employed today by fans at Scottish-English football matches.

Mobile tower or sow, sometimes known as a penthouse. This was a portable construction covered with hides for the protection of the attackers, who were able to storm walls on the higher level, and attack with battering rams at the base.

Now the deadly game began. Two serious attempts to retake Berwick were made over the course of a week in the beginning of September 1319. The English troops almost managed to scale the walls at their first attempt, which caused a degree of panic among some of the defenders who fled to the castle for safety. When discipline was re-asserted the Scots defended the walls strongly, and the scaling ladders were knocked to the ground. The walls were not high at certain sections of the defences, for a spearman, admittedly with a twelve-foot or longer spear, could strike at a defender's face. The English brought in their machines called sows. These were large, tall, movable timber constructions with protective roofs and sides. Under the protection, attackers using huge tree trunks capped with iron heads, would try to breach the wall at the base. Also, by ladders within the framework, men could arrive at the top, level with defenders on the walls. The fighting would be gory and fierce, with arrows, cross-bow bolts, and heavy missiles making it dangerous for anyone showing themselves above the defensive parapets. This attack failed for the lack of sows, and more siege engines were ordered to be brought from Bamburgh and further south. Later, the siege engines were very effective and in a subsequent attack, it was only through the use of John Crabbe's machine, a type of crane which could hurl missiles and

huge bundles of flaming faggots, that the siege engines were destroyed. When one sow was destroyed the cry went up 'the sow has farrowed' for the attackers fled from the burning assault tower, like piglets being born. In addition to the close quarter fighting, machines called ballistas or mangonels would be launching huge stones, weighing up to 5cwt, into the town. Basically, these were giant catapults, which though perhaps not having great accuracy, nevertheless could cause tremendous damage when fired into a besieged town.

Edward's ships now came near the walls, and one fully rigged ship came close in, being towed or propelled by men in small boats rowing with all their might. The big ship was full of armed men, and lashed to one of the masts high in the rigging, was a ship's boat. Extending from the boat was a makeshift drawbridge, which was to allow the attackers to surge across on to the walls. The defence was so spirited that they were repulsed, and as the tide began to ebb the ship grounded. A large force issued out of the town and quickly set fire to the ship, so that many aboard were killed or fled. Crabbe's crane was hurling boulders among the other ships causing great damage, especially to the small rowing barges which were bringing the ships near the wall. The writer of this account (Barbour) seems to be in no doubt about the location of these savage encounters, for he writes: 'And pressyt thain rycht fast to tow, hyr by the brighous to the wall', i.e. they rowed hard to tow the ship, by the Bridge-house to the wall. So it is likely this incident took place somewhere near the west end of what is now called Love Lane, for the old bridge was located in that area, and there would be a defensive barrier or 'Brighous' at the northern end of the bridge. In fact the bridge did not extend across the river, for it had been mostly destroyed by a flood some years earlier. The ships withdrew, but the landward area suffered repeated assaults which were driven back. The most serious was an attack on the drawbridge at the top of the Marygate, when it was burned, an attempt being made to fire the gate itself, but men issuing from the castle came to the help of the town garrison and the attack was repulsed.

So ended the siege of Berwick. Edward withdrew his defeated forces and the town remained in the hands of the Scots for the next fourteen years. Eight years after the siege, Edward II was deposed and murdered at Berkeley Castle in Gloucestershire, either by or at the behest of his wife. He met a particularly brutal death, by having a red hot wire or poker thrust into his rectum. The crown now passed to his fifteen years old son who, as Edward III, would come back to torment and take Berwick in 1333.

In the years that followed, Berwick's exports of wool increased considerably, especially to Flanders, Scotland's greatest ally. The Flemish ships had made repeated attacks on English shipping, stealing their cargoes which included wool destined for Germany and Flanders. The Fleming, John Crabbe, who was credited with saving Berwick with his war machines, was one of the principal pirates, and he and his ships were active, and his reputation as a privateer was well established, before he figures in Berwick's history. The ships plying the North Sea had 'castles' fitted fore and aft for defence against boarders, hence the term fo'c'sle for the present day fore-part of a merchant ship, being derived from 'fore-castle'. Many ships would be round-hulled and clinker-built, with one or perhaps two sails.

However much Scotland and Berwick prospered, there was still no recognition by the English King of Scotland's legitimate claim to be an independent nation. England's prosperity at this time suffered a decline, due to the failure of crops and disease in cattle, and the nobles were weary for peace; in 1323 a truce was declared. It was supposed to be for thirteen years,

but of course it did not last that long, and in any case the Scots continued their raiding in the north of England. In one raid the young Edward III was nearly captured by the Scots who inflicted a defeat on his men, and caused Edward to weep 'tears of vexation'.

Eventually, a peace treaty was drawn up recognizing King Robert's rightful status, and stipulating that Edward III would give up any claim to Scotland, for which he would receive £20,000 in silver, to be handed over in three instalments at Tweedmouth. Shortly afterwards, King Robert died of leprosy (1329), having charged his trusted friend Sir James Douglas to carry his heart in battle against the 'infidel'. Douglas commissioned a fine silver case, beautifully enamelled, and in this the King's heart was placed. This Sir James wore round his neck always. Then with a noble company of knights and squires, he embarked on a ship at Berwick which was to take them to Spain, en route for the Holy Land. Eventually, Robert's heart came back to Scotland and was buried in Melrose Abbey. Recently, it was re-interred there, and is now marked with a memorial stone.

Another ship, outward bound from Berwick in the year 1328, undoubtedly set out on a happier voyage. Destined for Flanders, it carried one Peter Machenar who had a lengthy shopping list ordered by the royal household. A banquet was to be held in Berwick to celebrate the betrothal ceremony of David (the late King Robert's son and heir apparent) and Joan, young sister of Edward III. David was four and Joan was seven! This arranged marriage was designed to hold together the fragile framework of peace between the two nations, and Berwick was the place where the union would take place. The town would play host to all the dignitaries and would share in the merriment and feasting.

Machenar was to purchase everything from pots and pans for the cooks, to cloth and fur for all the attendant servants and soldiers, who would be attired in a manner which would reflect the grandeur of the occasion. Needless to say there was a large order of wine on the list (20 hogsheads, equivalent to more than 7,000 present-day bottles). Also ordered were 200lb of sweets and confections – Belgium even then must have been well known for its confections – large quantities of honey and mustard, and every conceivable spice from canella to cinnamon, and galangal to ginger. Twenty oxen and 400 sheep, all locally reared, were to be slaughtered, and for the fish course no doubt there would be Tweed salmon, but there were certainly 2,200 eels from Flanders. Minstrels were engaged to entertain the company and gifts were made to some of the guests, including £180 to the Flemish engineer who had helped to save Berwick, John Crabbe. This was a very large sum which in those days could buy more than 500 oxen. Money was handed over for repairs to the walls, although one account implies that boisterous guests knocked down a churchyard wall! The festivities carried on for a very long time after the actual wedding ceremony, but eventually the bridal couple set out on the North road and the guests departed.

The uneasy peace was to be rudely shattered, for there was disaffection among certain Scottish barons as well as English nobles. Many of the Scottish houses held large estates in England, and just as many of the English lords held large estates in Scotland. These they had lost, due to the peace treaty between England and Scotland (Northampton, 1328). With the help of these disinherited nobles, Toom Tabard's son Edward Balliol was crowned King of Scotland, and the young David and his Queen, who had been married in Berwick, were forced into exile in France.

Minstrels in a production of The Merry Wives of Windsor, *performed on the Elizabethan Walls in 1993.*

The battles and guerrilla raids which followed between the two factions in Scotland allowed Edward III of England to move. He declared war – his first target was Berwick, and so once again the English armies moved north to confront the strongly garrisoned town. Edward III was determined not to fail as his father had in 1319, and so the preparations were thorough. Great siege engines, made in Yorkshire, were brought by ship along with the huge stones they would fire at the town. Supplies to support his armies were brought up, everything from hay to horseshoes, and beans to bows and arrows. The siege of Berwick began on 4 April 1333. A first attempt to take the town by a frontal attack failed, as did a naval attack, the ships being burned and driven back to sea. Edward arrived in the first weeks of May to take charge of the operations, which he conducted from his headquarters in Tweedmouth. He determined on a strict blockade which was to last three months, at the end of which time the inhabitants were ravaged by hunger. The battle which eventually determined the outcome occurred at Halidon Hill on 19 July 1333. Before that, Scottish hostages were executed on the orders of Edward, who claimed the Scots had not fulfilled the terms of a convention. It may seem strange to us now, but that word convention encompassed strange rules of chivalry, whereby opposing parties would agree terms of battle. In this case, the garrison agreed to surrender, unless relieved by Scottish armies before the chosen date, 20 July, and hostages were handed over as evidence of good intent. On the Tweedmouth side of the river, just through the arches of the railway bridge, is a grassy knoll, known today as Hang-a-Dyke Neuk, where the hostages reputedly were hanged, including it is said, one of the sons of Sir Alexander Seton, warden of Berwick.

The Scottish army under Sir Archibald Douglas had tried to draw Edward's troops to Bamburgh Castle where his Queen was but, not succeeding, Sir Archibald returned, crossed the Tweed by Yarrow Ford and encamped his troops somewhere north of Halidon Hill. This hill is a natural defensive feature commanding views over the whole area including the Tweed valley, and on the hill the English took their position. On the north side of the hill is Bogend, aptly named, for this marshy area is where the Scots had to struggle through to meet the enemy on 19 July. Scottish history is littered with tales of disasters and this was certainly one,

The view from Halidon Hill looking towards Berwick and its bay, beyond which is Bamburgh Castle.

comparable it is said with the Battle of Flodden 180 years later. The English archers with their long bows slaughtered the Scots in their thousands; earls, barons and Scottish knights were killed in their hundreds, and at one stroke the Scottish nation was deprived of its leaders, including Sir Archibald Douglas, the Regent. A bizarre episode is recorded as occurring before the battle, when a Scotsman of huge stature, one Turnbull, challenged any person on the English side to fight with him in a single combat. Whether this was a 'winner takes all' gamble is not known, but Turnbull, who must have been something of a big-head, not only lost his head, but his left arm as well, when they were severed by the skilful swordsman who had accepted his challenge. Perhaps the Scots should have gone home at this juncture.

The next day, the castle and town of Berwick were surrendered to Edward, who resting there after the battle, made various gifts to the religious houses including the Cistercian nunnery (situated near Halidon Hill), which had been damaged during the war.

The Earl of March (keeper of the castle) was rewarded by Edward, which would suggest he must have been helpful to Edward and that his sympathies were not with the Scots. A cleansing of the town followed, with expulsion of Scottish merchants, clergy and burgesses, to be replaced by their English counterparts. Scottish monks ordered out of the town were canny enough to keep their English replacements talking long enough to enable them to remove all their valuables.

Later in the year Edward returned to Berwick and laid waste to the lands north of the Border. Berwick was once more the storehouse for his armies, and vast quantities of foodstuffs which could be stored were piled into granaries and cellars. Dried fish, cereals, pulses and wine were among the goods listed. Two windmills and two horse-mills were brought from Newcastle, these to grind the meal required for the troops, due to the incapacity of the

This interesting plaque on the Halidon Hill viewing point was installed by Berwick Rotary Club. It depicts the duel between Turnbull and his opponent before the battle. There is also a panoramic interpretation of the scene from Halidon Hill.

THE DUEL BEFORE THE BATTLE

existing mill at the castle and mills at Edrington, three miles west of Berwick, which were in need of repair.

Wars between the two nations went on into the mid-1350s. This repeated marching and warring in the south of Scotland and north of England resulted in a destabilized society, and for more than two centuries thereafter lawlessness persisted in the area, most notably in the form of armed plunderers who were to achieve their own niche in history as Border Reivers.

The winter of 1341/42 came, and there was a six-month truce. At Easter, Edward came to Berwick and leaders of both sides fraternized with each other. A jousting match was arranged – almost as if they could not do without fighting, or in present-day parlance, they needed the buzz of killing each other. The heats were drawn up and prizes decided. Twelve Scottish knights were entered on the lists along with twelve English knights. After three days, the full-time score of killings was Scots 2, English 1. William Ramsay got a prize for best performance! A spear went clean through his helmet into his head, and his condition seemed so serious he was given absolution by the priest. His brother Alexander, however, put his foot on William's helmet and (no doubt with some force) pulled out the spear, whereupon a minute or two later William rose up and said he would 'ayl na-thyng' (he ailed not!). The Earl of Derby was greatly impressed, saying 'Lo! Stout hearts of men!', further saying that this had been a great tournament.

Edward Balliol, who had seized the Scottish crown some years before, was now hated by the Scots, for he had signed away possessions to Edward III of England. Truces, skirmishes and peace negotiations came and went, but Berwick was the only prize the English King still held. Now David Bruce, rightful King of Scotland, re-appeared from exile in France with an army, which wasted no time in raiding and plundering in Northumberland and Durham. The castle at Wark-on-Tweed was attacked by David, and saved only by urgent appeals to King Edward from the Countess of Salisbury whose husband owned the castle. Edward came to the rescue of the Countess and her castle, and according to the gossip of the time became smitten with her, although she was his first cousin. The story of the institution of the Order of the Garter at Wark probably originates from this time, but its authenticity cannot be assured. The story, for lovers of romance, is that during a ball to celebrate the occasion, the garter of the Countess became detached and titters among the courtiers were heard. Edward picked it up with some

Wark on Tweed castle as it might have looked in the sixteenth century. This is part of an interesting interpretation panel placed at Wark by English Heritage, Wark Estate and Northumberland County Council.

gallantry and said, '*Honi soit qui mal y pense*' (Evil to him who evil thinks), which remains the motto of the Order of the Garter to this day.

Edward III was still claiming the throne of France, and war broke out between England and France when the French invaded Gascony, Edward's possession. The war was to last for one hundred years, but a major battle occurred in 1346 when the English decisively won the battle of Crécy. This battle is notable for the use of cannon, the first occasion in which artillery was used in field warfare. This event would subsequently have a significant bearing on Berwick's fortifications, but that was still some way off. At this time, the walls, towers, parapets and battlements in Berwick were being repaired, and as there were nineteen towers in the old walls all connected with underground passages through the defensive mounds behind the walls, there was plenty to be done to ensure their strength. King Edward, anxious to keep Berwick, made concessions to the Berwick merchants to encourage trade, and even allowed the Scots to come into the town and transact business. The Bishop of Durham, who was being greedy in exacting heavy tolls on goods crossing the river, received orders from the King to cease imposing his levies forthwith.

Perhaps Edward loosened the controls too much for his own good, for in 1355 in October, the Scots, heady with success from their raids in the north of England, decided it was time to retake Berwick. A fleet of ships came in to the Greenses haven, and men scaled the walls near the Cowgate. Killing the captain of the town and other knights of the garrison, the Scots soon took the town. Those inhabitants who could, fled for safety to the castle or perhaps across the river by boat.

Edward left France when the news reached him, and even without any delay it was not until the middle of January that he arrived at Berwick Castle which his men still held. One account says that the captain of the castle, had great experience in sieges, and had in his company miners, whom he set to work to make an underground passage from the castle into the town. This mention of underground passages may account for the folklore stories recounted even yet in Berwick, of tunnels leading from cellars in West Street to the castle, of which there is no evidence, but yet may have some foundation in fact.

In any case, the Scots realized their peril and withdrew. Whether they knew the tunnellers were at work is not known, but an effective method of detection at this time was to place jars of water on the ground at intervals, and if the water rippled it was due to underground vibration. No doubt Berwick's buildings would suffer from the attentions of the Scots before they left, but that was as nothing to the retribution Edward exacted all over the south of Scotland. Raiding as far as Edinburgh, he burned many towns and caused great hardship. Thereafter this grisly episode was known as the Burnt Candlemas, for it happened at the time of the Scottish quarter day (Candlemas), 2 February.

King David II of Scotland was, at this time, a prisoner of Edward III having been captured in 1346 at a battle near Durham (Neville's Cross). Eventually he was released in 1357 after eleven years' captivity. For a large part of the time he was captive, negotiations took place in Berwick for his release, and eventually he was brought to Berwick by bishops and nobles of England and handed over to the care of their counterparts in Scotland. A large sum of ransom money was to be paid for his freedom, the instalments to be handed over at Berwick. Edward Balliol, his rival, was by this time abandoned by his supporters and eventually resigned all claims to the Scottish crown. In 1371 David's nephew Robert II became King on the death of his uncle. For the next hundred years Scotland as a nation and the Stewart dynasty as rulers would consolidate their position, and this line would lead to the Union of the Crowns in 1603.

In the second half of the fourteenth century, war, the great decimator of people and nations, gained an ally when the spectre of the Black Death stalked the land. It is possible that more people died from the plague than were killed by soldiers, and Berwick was not immune. Being a port where flea-bearing rats could come from ships and would multiply, and also being a closely packed town with insanitary conditions, an outbreak was inevitable. The plague had been known in the sixth century and it recurred numerous times in the three centuries following the initial outbreak in 1349. In the fourteenth century of which we write, while no statistics are available for Berwick, it is reckoned that between a third and a half of the inhabitants of these isles died. Land was uncultivated and though warring practically ceased at these times, Berwick was impoverished. Again the walls were receiving attention under the jurisdiction of the Deputy Governor of Berwick, Richard Tempest, and though Edward made concessions to the burgesses to encourage trade, all was not well.

In 1378 the castle was taken by robbers of the Scottish March (who probably came from the area which is now Berwickshire). They were soon captured by the Earl of Northumberland and his forces, which included his son Henry Hotspur. Most of the robbers were killed and the

The congested aspects of a town constrained within walls are well illustrated by this roofscape, photographed in the early 1960s from Berwick Town Hall roof. Many of these buildings have been demolished.

castle was back in English hands. The King of England was now the ten-year-old Richard II, Edward III his grandfather having died the previous year. A few years later, Berwick became a duty-free town, courtesy of Richard, for the tax on wine and the equivalent of VAT on goods was removed, but these impositions remained in force for the rest of England.

Berwick Castle seems to have been taken twice by the Scots in the early years of Richard's reign, and mention is made of the burning of Berwick so it is possible that yet again Berwick found itself in the cockpit of war not once but twice. In 1388 the Scots defeated the English at the battle of Otterburn, but in 1402 the English defeated the Scots at Homildon Hill near Wooler, and so it went on – truces broken, truces remade. At the end of the fourteenth century the famous Harry Hotspur was Assistant Governor of Berwick, his father the Duke of Northumberland (Henry Percy) being Warden of the East and West Marches, while Henry IV was on the throne of England. Though the Duke of Northumberland had conspired to set Henry IV on the throne, it was not long before both he and his son were complaining that they were not being paid enough!

The King decided that Berwick Castle should not be held by the Duke who was conspiring against him, nor that of Alnwick. Refused entry at Alnwick Castle by the captain in charge, Henry IV marched to Berwick and firing a large cannon demolished a tower whereupon the garrison surrendered the keys.

Later Percy returned with his 'heavy squad', gained possession of the castle and town and handed over the keys to the Scots who promptly sacked the town and burnt the houses. Later that year (1405), the town received compensation of 1,000 marks to repair the damage once the Scots had gone. Percy was killed in battle, having joined forces with Scotland, and part of his body was brought to Berwick and suspended in a public place, to denote his disgrace as a traitor.

King Henry IV appointed his son John as Warden of the Marches with the governorship of Berwick. In 1409 John, aged twenty, showed his mettle by writing to his father deploring the weakness of the walls, gates and bridges in Berwick (the bridges were those which connected the castle and the town and included drawbridges). He stressed that his soldiers had been suffering and were famishing, and if they left the town to forage for food, they were attacked and taken prisoner. John wrote imploring his father on two further occasions, telling him the walls were level with the ground in one place for more than 300 yards, and in another for 200 yards. He requested cannons, ammunition and victuals, warning that unless he received them, he could not defend the town. All this was despite using his own money to the extent of £13,000.

John would no doubt have been greatly pleased when, in 1413, he was relieved of his burden. His father's successor Henry V filled the office by making his son, the Duke of York, Governor of Berwick. In turn he was succeeded by Henry Percy, son of Harry Hotspur, who had cannon, ballistae and torments sent to Berwick. Torments were huge catapults, where the ropes of fibre or hair were twisted to gain the propulsion necessary to fire projectiles. He also saw to the repairs of the castle and defences, and so successful was he in his efforts that when the Scots again assaulted Berwick with a considerable force in 1421, they were repulsed. Later this assault was to be known as the 'Dirten Raid' (a modern equivalent might be the 'Crap Raid'!), for it was a complete failure.

The name of Harry Hotspur provided the inspiration for the title of a popular boys' magazine which flourished for more than fifty years. It was published by D.C. Thomson of Dundee and provided a weekly diet of stories of derring-do, which were well written and used a wide vocabulary, thus encouraging generations of schoolboys to appreciate the written word.

Robert II of Scotland had been succeeded by his son Robert III, a cripple and a weak ruler. He, in turn, was succeeded by James I who had been a captive of the English for fourteen years. He was now allowed, in 1424, to take his rightful position on the Scottish throne. This, however, was at some considerable cost to his exchequer, for he had undertaken to pay what was in effect ransom money. Some of this came to Berwick to pay wages of the soldiers and the cost of repairs to the castle and town. James I embarked on social and legislative reform and having been educated in England had become a man of scholarly tastes. His talents in poetry are

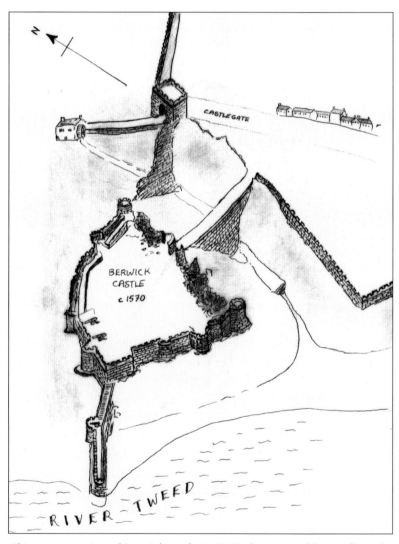

This representation of Berwick castle in 1570 shows crumbling walls at the rear, although most of the defences are in good condition. Entrance on the east side was by a bridge, the position of which approximates to the railway station carriageway today.

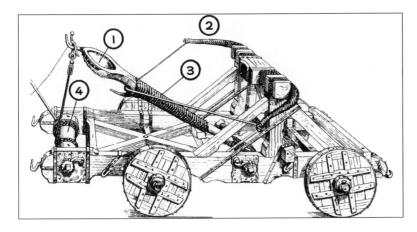

A torment or catapult. The missile placed at (1) is thrown by the spring (2) when the lever (3) – drawn down by the winch – is released.

Riders crossing the Magdalen Fields during the Riding of the Bounds ceremony on 1 May.

remembered for his well-known poem *The King's Quhair*, but he will probably be best remembered for his Act of 1424 which specifically stated 'that nae man sall play at the fut ball'. He was murdered in 1437, but not we think by disgruntled footballers!

Anglo-Scottish relations remained strained and truces, raids and counter-raids continued in the all too familiar pattern. Cattle and horses were taken by the Scots in a raid in 1433, but eventually both sides, wearied by the continual fighting, signed a truce in 1438, which lasted in excess of seven years and saw the first mention of the liberties of Berwick – i.e. where the garrison and citizens could safely move about, graze their cattle and gather fuel. In other words the safe boundaries were outlined, which are still ridden today in the ceremony of Riding the Bounds on 1 May each year.

About this time, the Scots instituted a telegraphic service throughout the borders, which would warn of English incursions. Its name 'Bale Fire' was literally that, for depending on the scale of the threat, one bale of straw or wood, to four bales were set alight simultaneously on hill tops. Four bales denoted the maximum warning of a large invasive force. It was the Scots, however, under James II who threatened and in 1455 came close to Berwick, but on a show of strength by the English troops they withdrew.

CHAPTER 4
Roses, Stewarts and Tudors

A strange turn of events now took place which returned Berwick to the Scots. Henry VI of England, the Lancastrian, was fighting for his survival, against Edward, the Yorkist, in the quaintly named Wars of the Roses. The Yorkists were victorious in 1461, and Edward became Edward IV of England. Henry, defeated, arrived in Berwick with his wife and son, then departed to throw himself on the mercy of James III of Scotland. James' father, James II, had been killed by the bursting of a cannon at the siege of Roxburgh Castle the previous year. Although only a child (James was ten) he received Henry in a kindly manner and promised him succour. In return, Berwick town and castle were given to the Scots. They were to remain in their hands for twenty-one years, when Berwick would finally be lost to them.

Henry VI's French wife, Margaret, the daughter of the King of Anjou, displayed considerable courage in fighting her husband's wars. She went to France and obtained help from Louis XI, King of France. With her newly acquired troops, she sailed from France only to be caught in a storm. She is supposed to have landed at Berwick, but only in a coracle, many of her ships having been driven ashore at Bamburgh. Some of her army, after being forced back from Alnwick Castle, came to Berwick in fishing boats. Dunstanborough Castle, 25 miles south of Berwick, was five times taken and retaken at this time, and became ruinous.

Berwick, now in Scottish hands once more, was paying the garrison and officers of the town and castle their wages from the customs they collected. This was just as before when the English were masters. Some of the bailies of Berwick who had incurred the King's displeasure, were put into prison at Blackness Castle on the Forth, or Dumbarton Castle in the west, but occasionally in Berwick Castle.

Refortifying the town went on apace. New strong walls were built, victuals stored and even war engines were made in the town, notably 'sows' which were no strangers to Berwick. The expected retaliation came when the victorious Edward IV decided Berwick should not have been given away by his defeated rival Henry VI. He attacked in 1481 but so stout was the Scots defence that he had to withdraw.

An event at Lauder, Berwickshire, in the next year was to change the destiny of Berwick. James III's own brother, Alexander Duke of Albany, wanted the crown of Scotland, and he allied himself with Edward IV of England. Such is the perfidy of men greedy for power, that brother would turn on brother. The whole fabric of the interwoven story of Scotland and England is pierced by such episodes and it is difficult to tease out the individual threads.

While making for the Border to deal with the English invaders, King James was ambushed by some of his own disaffected nobles at Lauder. His advisers were hanged over Lauder Bridge, and the king was taken to Edinburgh Castle and imprisoned. The chief conspirator was Archibald Douglas who earned the sobriquet 'Bell the Cat' for his willingness to strike the first blow (after the fable of 'The Cat and the Mice'). The Scottish army, demoralized by the loss

The Red Lion Hotel was an important coaching inn dating from the eighteenth century. It stood where Woolworths is situated today. On the extreme left, a lady is standing at the door of Archibald Suthren's hairdresser's shop. On the extreme right is Joseph Ewart's antique furniture shop, while the shop with the horse and cart in front is that of William Scott, flour and meal merchant. This view dates from around 1905.

of their leader, dispersed, and Berwick fell to the English, whether by force (for there was a large English army at the gates), or whether by settlement is not clear, but Berwick was to be an English possession from that day to this.

Edward IV of England was succeeded by his son Edward V (aged thirteen) who reigned for three months before being smothered in the Tower of London, possibly by his uncle. A missive signed by the young king, addressed to 'George Porter, Master Carpenter of our Works in our Town and Castle of Berwick', orders him to obtain the best timber from Essex. This was for buildings to be started in Berwick by order of the King. Porter was authorized to obtain the carts, workers and ships necessary for the transport of the wood, and in the letter of authority, the poor little king refers to 'our dearest Uncle, the Duke of Gloucester'. 'Our dearest Uncle' was probably to be his murderer, who a year before had been at the gates of Berwick in charge of the large English army, and who subsequently became Richard III of England after his young nephew was killed.

Shakespeare cast Richard III as a deformed villain and ugly, so much so, that he has him say 'that dogs bark at me as I halt by them'. The opening line of the play 'Now is the winter of our discontent' could be applied to His Majesty's town of Berwick at this time, for trade had declined due to the destructive warring. The wool trade had largely disappeared, and although salmon was exported, this was a poor substitute in terms of wealth creation.

The garrison of course continued, and much of the business of the town was the supply of provisions and other necessities. The Earl of Northumberland was keeper of Berwick town and castle, and was paid to provide 600 soldiers for its defence, the soldiers being paid sixpence a day. Among the soldiers were Swiss mercenaries who had a banner bearer, a piper and a drummer ('Baner-berer, Weveler and Taboret'), and they were paid sixpence a day above their wage. The garrison was to be strengthened by another 1,200 soldiers, if danger threatened.

Richard III met his death at the Battle of Bosworth Field, defeated by Henry Tudor who as first of the Tudor monarchs became Henry VII. He was unusual in that he died in bed in marked contrast to most of his predecessors. In 1503 his eldest daughter Margaret was married to James IV of Scotland. James was in his late twenties and Margaret in her early teens, a difference of age of about fifteen years. Her progress north to meet her bridegroom-to-be is well documented. In July, she and her retinue arrived at Belford and 'bayted' i.e. ate a meal (prepared for her by the 'Capittayne of Berwick'). One hundred men at arms arrayed in fine livery and well horsed, arrived from Berwick to escort the entourage to the town. Nearing Berwick, a large number of guns were fired in salute, and Margaret, changing her apparel for something more befitting the occasion, was ready to be received at the south end of the bridge. Similarly at the north end, near the gate which defended the bridge entrance, soldiers with halberds and minstrels playing their instruments, stood alongside all the dignitaries of the town ready to welcome her.

Margaret was then conveyed to the castle, where the 'Capittayne's' wife, Lady Darcy, looked after her for the next two days. During her stay, Margaret was treated to such delights as bear-baiting (the setting of dogs on a chained bear), chase coursing, 'and other gentlemanly sports'!

Lamberton Toll, c. 1890. This was the nearest Scottish ground to Berwick and it was renowned for irregular marriages. Eloping couples could cross the Border and after a short ceremony conducted by a bogus minister or priest, would receive a certificate stating they had been married. At one time, the toll house displayed a notice 'Ginger Beer sold here and marriages performed.'

Ferry-boats landing their passengers from Berwick at the Spittal landing stage, c. 1903. Between 1300 and 1500 no bridge existed between Berwick and the south side of the river, and ferries were in use for foot passengers, and wherries (barge-like boats) used for horses and carts.

She then departed for Lamberton Kirk, where she was entrusted to the Scottish royal party. Some 2,000 persons accompanied the future Queen to the Scottish border, and two or three days later she met her husband-to-be, King James IV, in Edinburgh. She was processed through the streets riding pillion on the King's horse to Holyrood Palace, where the marriage ceremony took place.

William Dunbar, an itinerant preaching friar of the Franciscan order and also a famous Scottish poet, wrote a poem entitled *The Thistle and the Rose* to celebrate the occasion. Sir Walter Scott wrote that Dunbar was a poet unrivalled by any that Scotland had produced.

The mention of the bridge which spanned the river between Tweedmouth and Berwick is interesting, because it must have been of fairly recent construction. An Italian writer from this time gives credit to Henry VII for building it, as previously, for almost two centuries, there was no bridge, and ferries or fords provided for passages across the river.

There was peace on the Border, but it was a brittle peace. James IV of Scotland embarked on an arms race and spent massive sums on building up a navy, the largest and best-known ship being the *Great Michael* which was the biggest ship in the world at 240ft long. This aroused great suspicion in the mind of King Henry VIII of England who had succeeded to the throne in 1509 on the death of his father.

A dispute arose about a Flemish ship which had been taken into Berwick, where the goods intended for Scotland were impounded. Scotland was in turn told to return English goods taken by pirates operating out of Scottish ports and so it went on. Scotland was now asked by her old ally France for help. England was attacking France from one side and the Pope and his allies were attacking from the other, and France stood alone. James sent his warships to aid the French King, and ordered his army to muster and march south to invade England.

James IV crossed the border and took Norham, Wark, Etal and Ford castles, using a number of new bronze guns in the attacks. Each gun had to be drawn by up to thirty-six oxen, with eight or nine drivers and twenty labourers with spades, picks, shovels and ropes – a tremendous undertaking. He then moved to take up his position on Branxton Hill, declining an invitation from the Earl of Surrey in charge of the smaller English army to engage forces

An annual remembrance service is held at the Flodden memorial each year on the anniversary of the battle (9 September 1513), when Scotland lost the flower of its nobility, and its King, James IV.

on Milfield Plain, and so the die was cast for the fateful Battle of Flodden. A feinting move by Surrey's troops led James to order the advance, and the fifteen foot spears of the Scots were found wanting against the savage English bills, which had hooks as well as blades. James was hacked to pieces along with his nobles, and it is said 10,000 Scots were killed. James's body was brought to Berwick and shipped to Newcastle, whence it went to Richmond. The fine guns (culverins) made of bronze were brought to Berwick to be taken by land to Newcastle, but permission to cross the bridge over the Tweed at Berwick was refused, possibly because damage might be done to the wooden bridge. Eventually the cannon were shipped from Berwick some nine years after the Battle of Flodden. They had been kept in a storehouse on the Walls Green then moved to the Maison Dew (*sic*) quay where a special crane lifted them aboard a ship, which took them to the Tower of London. As for the much vaunted Scottish navy – it was sold to the French and included in the sale was the mighty warship, the *Great Michael*, which had so awed Henry VIII.

The Homes of Wedderburn had taken part in the battle of Flodden, and Sir David and his eldest son George were killed. David junior succeeded to the title Lord Home, and was chamberlain of Scotland when the Duke of Albany was Governor of Scotland and Regent to the infant son of James IV. Albany, determined to get rid of Home, had him and his brother tried and beheaded on trumped-up charges of treason and 'treacherous inactivity in the battle' (of Flodden). Some of the Homes were now in the pay of the Berwick captain and were lodged at Caw Mills (Edrington) four miles from Berwick, where they supported the English garrison by raiding against their own countrymen, the Scots. A Frenchman who had been appointed Warden in place of the Homes in the Eastern March of Scotland, was unwise enough to let himself be captured by the Homes. They cut his head off, tied his long hair in a plait and hung it from the saddle as a grisly trophy, such was their bitterness against the Scots. Later the Homes changed sides yet again, but this is a story typical of these troubled times. Truces made and broken, allegiances, first with one and then the other – this rapid switching of loyalties was all about lust for power and position, not to mention wealth. The wealthy titled Border landowners of today are the product of this chicanery, violence and brutality.

In Berwick, a new tower was being built on the sands (near Coxon's Tower), but the castle and ramparts were in an enfeebled state, and the threat of the Duke of Albany coming to attack the town was ever present. Nevertheless numerous raids into the borders were made by English troops under the command of the Earl of Surrey (Duke of Norfolk), son of the commander of the English army at Flodden. Kelso and Jedburgh were burned and the abbeys destroyed. Albany in turn was rampaging through the Border country, and the castle of Wark again came under a very severe assault. In 1524 Scots attacked traders and others going to a fair in Berwick (the May Fair?) and took spoil and prisoners, and later an attack by the English under Sir John Fenwick did likewise. A peace treaty was in force, but complaints between the two countries continued, usually about raids but also about traders and their shipments of goods from Berwick.

As always, the state of the defences pre-occupied George Lawson who was not only Master

Coxon's Tower. This was a look-out tower but also a gun tower with a sloping parapet allowing defenders to fire down at the enemy.

Carpenter, Bridge Master, and Master of the Ordnance (guns), but also Burgh Treasurer, Customs Officer etc. The walls were being undermined by the sea, and the storehouses, brewhouses and mills were much decayed. The tower of the White Wall was damaged by the action of the water, and the wooden bridge had been damaged by ice floes.

Treaties were signed in 1528 and 1534, but raids by the Berwick garrison continued, burning and destroying in Teviotdale and the Merse. Places like Oldhamstocks, Cockburnspath, Ayton and Dunglass were burned, and thousands of sheep and 'noyte' (cattle) taken. All these raids were done with the connivance of Henry VIII. Incursions into Scotland from Berwick on two occasions in 1542 were harrying raids, being attempts by Henry VIII to turn the screw tighter and force Scotland to turn its face away from France, its old ally.

James V died in 1542 leaving a daughter just a week old – the future Mary Queen of Scots. Henry VIII negotiated a treaty of marriage for the infant Mary to marry his son Edward, aged five. Mary was to be delivered to Berwick when she reached the age of twelve so that the marriage could take place. This settlement was repudiated by the Estates of Scotland (Scottish Parliament).

Henry, incensed by this reversal of his scheme, decided on direct action. He ordered the Earl of Hertford to invade Scotland and make it a desolate land, and this he did. Edinburgh was burned, and villages and towns on both sides of the Forth were razed as was Haddington, Leith and Dunbar. In an account of Hertford's campaign, printed in London in 1544, is the description of the firing of Dunbar. The defenders had gone to bed after a night of watching, thinking Hertford's men had departed, 'and in their first sleeps [Hertford] closed in with fire – the men, women and children were suffocated and burnt.... On the 18th May, the whole [of Hertford's] army entered Berwick and ended this voyage with the loss of scarcely forty of the King's Majesty's people, thanks be to our Lord.' The account goes on: 'The same day, at the same instant that the army entered into Berwick, our whole fleet and navy of ships, which we sent from us at Leith, arrived before Berwick, as God would be known to favour our master's cause.'

Berwick and its garrison were not idle during this time. The Governor of Berwick, Lord Eure, and his son Sir Ralph, along with others including one Sir Bryant Layton, sacked various towns and villages including Duns and Hutton, slew many and took cattle and corn in large quantities. Monasteries, religious houses, mills, hospitals – all received the same savage treatment. The abbeys of Kelso, Melrose, Dryburgh and Eccles were reduced to heaps of rubble.

The main perpetrators of these Border savageries, Sir Ralph Eure and Sir Bryant Layton, gloated over the havoc they had created. Subsequently, they met their death at the Battle of Ancrum Moor, when enraged locals joined with the forces of the Scottish Earl of Angus to defeat the English marauders. A gravestone on the site commemorates a heroine of the battle in these words.

'Fair Maiden Lilliard lies under this stane
Little was her stature but muckle was her fame;
Upon the English loons she lade many thumps
And when her legs were cuttit off
She fought upon her stumps.'

A composite picture of a town wait and, in the background, the Town Hall. The building on the left is now Park's shoe shop and on the right is Callers Pegasus travel agents. The tradition of waits entertaining the Mayor and Corporation with music at functions existed for about 400 years, only dying out in the first half of the nineteenth century. In 1731, a dispute between the garrison and the guild resulted in the waits not being allowed to stand and play on the New Gate Head (Scotsgate) to welcome back the Mayoral party from the riding of the bounds. The waits supplemented their meagre salary of £7 per annum by serenading the citizens at Christmas. Appropriately, the last wait, James Wallace, who died in 1845, kept the Fiddle and Tambourine Inn on Shaw's Lane (Chapel Street).

The two chained bears and the wych-elm trees on the coat of arms relate in a punning way to Ber (for the bear) and Wick (for the tree). Berne in Switzerland also has a bear on its coat of arms, no doubt similarly derived from Ber in its name.

A romantic style of painting is evident in this representation of a beached Berwick smack on Tweedmouth strand. A rather short bridge is shown in the background with salmon fishers working in the centuries-old fashion. Thought to date from the early nineteenth century, it is unsigned.

Two Berwick smacks in full sail voyaging south with a brig in their wake. (Reproduced by kind permission of the artist Bryan Page)

This arrivals and departures board for Berwick smacks was displayed on the London quay in the early 1800s. It is now in the Berwick Museum, having been gifted by the Berwick Salmon Fisheries Co. who were the successors to the old Berwick Shipping Company, operators of the fast sailing ship service between Berwick and London.

The following SMACKS armed by *Government* with *Carronades &c.* belonging to the *Old Shipping Cº of Berwick* upon *Tweed, Sail* from the *Leith & Berwick Wharf* on *Sundays* and *Thursdays*, direct for *Berwick*, and have *Genteel* Accommodations for *Passengers*.

ARRIV'D		SAILS.
ALERT	Wᵐ Turner.	
LIVELY	Wᵐ Nesbitt.	
ALBION	Joˢ Jameson.	
BRITANNIA	Mᶜ Brown.	
SWALLOW	R Charles.	
TWEED	Jaˢ Finley.	
LONDON & BERᵏ	Wᵐᵈ Fleming	

A. LAURIE & Cº Wharfingers.

An evocative scene of warriors before a battle, the tension showing on their faces. This is as it may have been before the battle of Halidon Hill. (Unknown artist)

Although Berwick's walls were never tested during the Civil Wars, this re-enactment by the Civil War Society shows what it might have been like had the town resisted.

A splendid military tattoo takes place in September each year within the setting of the Barracks.

Over the gateway at the Barracks is this colourful coat of arms of 1717. It shows the French arms (top right quarter) and the Scottish, English and Irish arms. Also shown (bottom right quarter) are the German Hanoverian arms introduced by George I which includes the golden crown of Charlemagne.

Berwick Castle and White Wall of 1297.

Salmon fishers at work below Berwick's old bridge.

Early morning, with mist rising over the river.

Spittal promenade from the south.

A winter morning – looking down on the Quay Walls and Bridge.

In 1536 George Lawson, Bridge Master, reported, 'The ice this winter has endangered the bridge which is all of timber'. In 1608 it was reported 'the spate rose and brought the ice so fast [that] tenn pillars and eleven bayes was then thrust down.' This was the wooden bridge which was replaced by the present bridge (pictured).

Red pantiles were originally imported from Flanders, but these roofs would be tiled by locally-made pantiles possibly from the Tweedmouth pantilery or Low Cocklaw Tile Works.

Tweedmouth House, now a residential home, was originally the Virgin Inn where Tobias Smollet stayed in 1766. In his novel Humphrey Clinker *he writes, 'I have now reached the northern extremity of England, and see, close to my chamber window, the Tweed gliding through the arches of that bridge which connects this suburb to the town of Berwick.'*

An aerial view of 1985 showing the Town Hall steeple in scaffolding, and the Maltings as a roofless shell, also the old quayside and shipyard slipway.

Class A2 Pacific No. 60532 Blue Peter *steaming south from Berwick in October 1993.*

Berwick's four bridges. The Edwardian and Elizabethan defences to the east of the town are clearly discernible.

Poppies and the Pier.

Russian Dancers *by Degas. This painting is in the Berwick Museum and Art Gallery which also has nineteenth-century paintings by Gericault and Boudin.*

From a series called 'Famous Fights' published by D.C. Thomson & Co. in the 1930s and given free by the weekly boys' paper The Wizard. *The champion of the tournament according to the Wizard was the Scotsman Sir Patrick Grahame, who killed three English knights in the tournament at Berwick in the fourteenth century.*

Holy Trinity parish church, built 1650-52 during the time of Cromwell the Protector. Puritan in design, it originally had no altar and it has no steeple; nevertheless, Pevsner in his Buildings of England *considered it a building of quite exceptional architectural interest.*

This stained glass medallion shows Berwick's coat of arms and is in the parish church's west window which also incorporates Flemish roundels of the sixteenth century.

The castle of Lindisfarne on Holy Island (which dates from the sixteenth century) was transformed into a striking house by Sir Edward Lutyens for Edward Hudson, owner of Country Life. It now belongs to the National Trust and is open to the public.

Bamburgh Castle, built on a sheer-sided outcrop of the Whin Sill, was restored in the 1890s for Lord Armstrong, the armaments tycoon. There have been defensive works on this commanding site for more than 2,000 years, but the only battles now are those of the football teams.

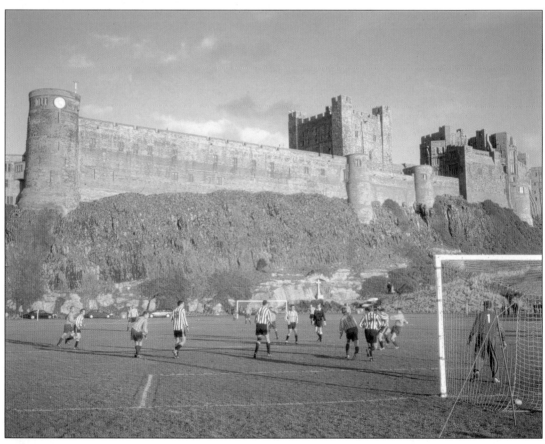

Norham Castle, chief northern stronghold maintained by the bishops of Durham. In the castle in 1290, Edward I deliberated on the successor to the Scottish throne.

The Union (or Chain) Bridge near Horncliffe connects England and Scotland over the River Tweed. It was the first suspension bridge for wheeled vehicles in Britain and was built in 1820. A launch taking visitors from Berwick to the Chain Bridge operates in the summer.

These spectacular cliffs a few miles north of Berwick are among the highest on the East Coast of Britain, rising a sheer 450ft above sea level at this point.

A survey of the Borders in 1544 refers to the fords of the River Tweed. Within the bounds of Berwick are the following crossings:

1. The lowest one enters the river near the Church of Tweedmouth and crosses to the water or shoregate of Berwick.
2. The bridge is next, which is 'suerly kept and garded'.
3. Berwick Stream – a little above the Castle.
4. South Yare – from Ord to the Castle fields.
5. The Nether Bells (where the border line goes north to Paxton Toll).

The bridge may have been 'suerly garded' but it was in a bad state of repair having been 'shaken by the passage of ordnance and warlike stores'.

Also shaken at this time was the Catholic faith of both England and Scotland, having been in a state of decline over the previous one hundred years. Corruption was widespread and the immorality of the clergy was well known. Cardinal Beaton of St Andrews had eight illegitimate children in his time, and later, a bastard son of James IV was made Archbishop of St Andrews at the age of eleven. Even in Iona, one of the nuns was the daughter of one of the monks. In her case, she really could give him the title of Father when addressing him!

Henry VIII was sympathetic to the Protestant cause, partly for reasons connected with his desire for a divorce, but mostly because of his increasing conviction that a nation should not be subservient to a foreign power, even if headed by the Pope. Thus the ground was fertile for preachers like John Knox, who was a leader in the Reformation cause. He arrived in Berwick in 1549 to further the Protestant movement in England, through the intervention of Edward VI, who had gained him his freedom from being a French galley slave. Edward VI had ascended the throne on the death of his father in 1547.

Knox's voice calling for people to repent no doubt made a profound impression. He was no stranger to temptation himself, however, for in a letter to his mother-in-law he wrote 'what I

A painting (c. 1827-29) thought to be the work of the Berwick artist Thomas Sword Good. In the distance is South Bells fishing shiel. The salmon coble pictured in the foreground probably belonged to the Yardford fishery. At this time there would be well over 100 such commercial fishing stations under the jurisdiction of the Tweed Fisheries Acts. Now there are four.

Lord's Mount artillery fort built by order of Henry VIII in 1540. In the distance is the Bell Tower built some forty years later, probably replacing a previous tower on the original Edwardian walls.

did standing in the cupboard in Alnwick, when I thought that no creature had been tempted as I was.' This conjures up a strange vision! John Knox stayed for two years in Berwick, preaching in the Holy Trinity church, i.e. the building which preceded the present church. The pulpit in the present-day church is reputed to be the one from which John Knox preached, and according to his own account he changed the bloodthirsty and quarrelsome soldiers into meek lambs!

About this time, an artillery fort was built at Lords Mount, near the Bell Tower, the substantial remains of which can be seen today. It has six vaulted gun casemates, each with vents to remove the smoke, and an upper floor with gun embrasures. For ordnance this fort had fifteen cannon plus hand arms. Accommodation for the men who would man the guns was provided and of course this required a kitchen, a well and a privy. Lords Mount was built at great cost (£10,000) and it was redundant within fifteen years. In the town, the streets were described as being so foul that in an emergency, soldiers could not pass through to man the walls. The toll-booth and prisons would also appear to have been in need of repair.

The Mayor of Berwick managed to get himself killed in 1554 by supporting the Herons against the Carrs, in a dispute regarding the ownership of Ford Castle. A contemporary report wryly states, 'Considering the enemy of Scotland we heve, God Knoweth, lytle neede of anye domestyque dissension amonges ourselves.'

Some three years later, the Scottish armies had been supplemented by some 7,000 French troops, for in 1557 Mary I of England (who had succeeded her brother Edward VI to the throne in 1553) had declared war against France, Scotland's old ally. A fort had been built at Eyemouth some years previously by the English, to guard the approach to England and Berwick, and was subsequently given up under the terms of the Treaty of Boulogne. Now the French, realizing that a fort at Eyemouth would block Berwick and make Scotland more secure, rebuilt the fort.

Thus it came about that some Berwick townspeople cutting hay on Halidon Hill were attacked by French troops from Eyemouth. Severe fighting ensued for although the workers in the field had been under the protection of some of the garrison, it needed reinforcements from Berwick to drive the French back to Eyemouth, with casualties said to be considerable.

Queen Elizabeth I now enters the stage, having succeeded to the English throne on the death of her sister in 1558. The port of Calais, the last English possession in France, was lost in that year, and Berwick was viewed as the equivalent of Calais, in that it was England's toehold in Scotland. So concerned was Elizabeth that she ordered that the new fortifications at Berwick (Elizabethan Walls) be proceeded with apace, the Edwardian Walls being abandoned. Elizabeth was Protestant, while her cousin Mary Queen of Scots was Catholic. Elizabeth was suspicious of Mary and her claim to the English throne. This coloured

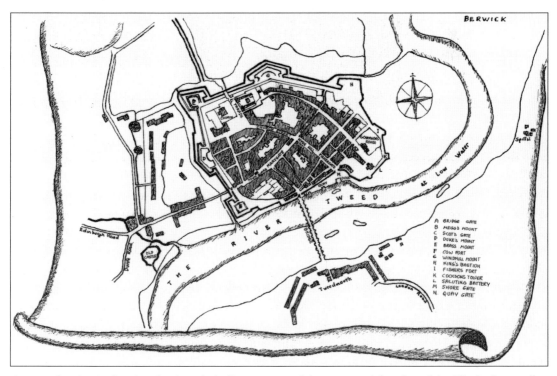

A map of c. 1769, showing the densely built-up nature of the town and the plan of the Elizabethan walls.

Players in the Maltings Community Theatre Co. progress like ghosts through the Shoregate, in Shakespeare's The Merry Wives of Windsor.

Elizabeth's outlook during all her reign, despite the Treaty of Edinburgh (1560), whereby the French agreed to withdraw from Scotland and recognize Elizabeth as Queen of England.

Berwick was victualled yet again and this time for 4,000 men 'out of season' and for 5,000 in the marching season – July to October. 1,500 labourers were sent to build up and finish the fortifications and put the place in order, which was a massive undertaking. The sixteenth century saw the development of artillery, and the new walls were built to take account of this. Military engineering at this time was being pioneered in Italy, and though Sir Richard Lee was the English expert who planned the new fortifications, on at least two occasions, an Italian expert, Giovanni Portinari, was called in for specific advice. Lucca in Italy has comparable walls to Berwick, being commenced some decades before Berwick, and the similarity is striking. The facing of the walls at Lucca is made up of some six million bricks, whereas the walls at Berwick are faced with stone, some of which undoubtedly came from the Edwardian walls which were now regarded as redundant. Lucca's walls are some 2 ½ miles long compared to Berwick's 1 ½ miles. The work on Berwick's walls lasted until 1570 and the total cost was nearly £130,000 – an average of £10,000 a year – a huge sum, and one which seriously depleted the Royal purse. The Walls

Looking along the curtain wall between Cumberland bastion and Brass bastion. The gun platforms and access tunnel entrance (on the right), and the high cavaliers on Brass bastion, are clearly defined.

at 22ft high are nothing like the height of the old medieval walls at 35ft, but they were designed to present less of a target to guns, with a tremendous depth of earth behind to absorb the impact. Projecting bastions were built in the shape of arrowheads to cover the defence of the walls, and also to allow guns to be mounted on top for offensive purposes. These bastions are linked with a strong curtain wall, and each bastion protected its adjoining bastion with cannons able to fire along the line of the wall. In front of the walls was a ditch with water, mostly shallow, but with a deep trench 12ft wide and 8ft deep in the middle, so that wading attackers would unwittingly find themselves out of their depths in the concealed moat. About seventy years later, earthen mounds were added to the tops of the walls to increase the protection against artillery, and today, with the exception of alterations to the gates of entrance, the walls are very much as they were when built.

The builders of the walls were not happy, for the captain in charge of the exchequer was being miserly with pay and rations, and he was probably lining his pockets with the money he saved. The men were being fed mostly on herring, red and white, which often were 'naughty' (i.e. they were off!), and were sometimes without pay for ten weeks, so they could not buy shirts and shoes. The weather would probably not be conducive to good health, for the biting winds and inadequate food would lay them open to disease. Certainly a lot of their superiors did not like the 'unagreeable' air of the town. Peregrine Bertie (Lord Willoughby) who was Governor at the end of the sixteenth century, wrote to William Cecil (first Lord Burghley) who was Queen Elizabeth's chief advisor, wanting to be retired from this 'accursed country whence the sun is so removed'.

Cecil was compelled to issue orders to install discipline among the thievish and ill-behaved garrison at this time – 'the soldiers cross over to Tweedmouth and daily fight' being one complaint. Death was to be the penalty for affrays at the gates, or for going from the walls after the watch-word was given. Beheading was the punishment for not giving warning of any ship or person coming in sight. Anyone sleeping on watch would be suspended in a basket over the walls 'with a can of drink in their hands', and there they would tarry (three days perhaps) until such time as the rope would be cut, when of course they would fall into the water.

Windmill Mount in winter conditions. In 1514, Sir Ralph Eure replied to Henry VIII's invitation to take the deputyship of Berwick, saying 'I could not have health there because of the cold weather and the sea air, but I would gladly serve the King in any other part of the world.'

Nobody could play dice by night, except members of the Town Council, nor could they walk abroad after ten o'clock in summer and eight o'clock in winter, or whistle or sing or shout after the said hours on pain of four days' imprisonment. It was claimed that Berwick became almost devoid of vices after two preachers were made resident there, but the truth was more likely to be that the evil-doers were sent out of Berwick, for certainly 269 'abominable Damoselles' and some Scots were sent packing. The governor wrote 'I confess I am more apt to be a bumbailiff than I was thirty years past.' (A bumbailiff was a hot pursuer of debtors and other miscreants.)

No Scots were allowed in the garrison on pain of death, but nonetheless men of the garrison were always pleased when the Scots came to the Calf Hill with provisions to sell. Calf Hill was the area between Castle Terrace and the North Road, just behind the Toll House which stands at the junction of the two roads. There was even a proposal to build them a type of canteen so that in bad wintry weather, they could have something to eat and drink, and warm themselves at a fire. A new customs officer had to retire from his position when it was found he had been born in Scotland, and although brought up in England from an early age by his mother and English stepfather, he had to surrender his appointment.

If Berwick was devoid of vices, the same could not be said of Tweedmouth, which was the refuge and den of all 'disorderly people hanging on the garrison'. No doubt with the removal of the 269 'loose

A scene from The Merry Wives of Windsor *performed below Wellington Terrace. Behind the figure on the right is a vaulted chamber, which was at one time the base of a medieval tower on the Edwardian walls.*

Cumberland and Brass Bastions and Windmill Mount are seen in this aerial view, also the covered way and the Great Bulwark on the Snook. On a more modern note, the bus station has disappeared, being now replaced by the library and three shops fronting onto the Marygate.

ladies' from Berwick, business would be booming in Tweedmouth for the ladies of easy virtue. In Spittal, the inhabitants had descended like locusts on a boat which grounded on the Spittal side of the estuary. The cargo of dry fish and wheat disappeared overnight, along with all the fittings and furnishings of the ship. Two centuries later, Spittal was said to be 'almost wholly inhabited by sea-faring people, who used to be reckoned of peculiarly unaccommodating dispositions and boisterous manners'!

Work was continuing on the new walls, with considerable amounts of stone coming from the castle. This pink sandstone is easily recognizable today, where large sections near the Cow Gate show by their contrasting colour where the castle stone was used. Disagreements occurred between the engineers and the Italian experts who wanted the walls to be extended from Brass Mount to the cliffs above the sea. A compromise was reached, and a deep ditch was dug from the position of the old Cowgate across the Magdalene Fields to the cliff tops. This covered way or traverse, provided another line of defence and is clearly discernible today. Another point of controversy was whether the walls to the south of the town should keep to the high ground between Kings Mount and Megs Mount, but this idea was eventually dropped because the lower town contained the royal storehouses, and would thus be undefended against an attack from the river. There are traces of an old high wall, which may be part of this Cat Well Wall as it was named, and they may be seen from the roadway at Love Lane at

the back of a cobbled courtyard. There was every reason for continuing with building defensive walls, for Scotland was in anything but a stable state.

Mary Queen of Scots had been briefly married to the Dauphin, eldest son of the King of France (the Dauphin became King of France for one year before he died). After her husband's death she had to leave France, and came back to Scotland to take her rightful place on the throne. Mary was Catholic, while many of her subjects were Protestants, whose emotions were easily aroused by John Knox and his supporters, one of whom was Elizabeth I of England, who had of course a vested interest in stirring things up. Mary, however, had plans of her own, and one involved marrying her cousin Lord Darnley, a Catholic with a claim to the English throne. Mary soon tired of her husband and took a lover Rizzio, who subsequently was assassinated by Darnley in front of his heavily pregnant wife. The baby in the womb was to become James VI of Scotland and I of England. Later Darnley was killed when the house he was staying in at Kirk O'Field was blown up by James Hepburn, the Earl of Bothwell. Bothwell was charged and acquitted of the murder, but Mary was widely believed to have been an accessory, if not the instigator of the crime. Later, Bothwell, keeper of Liddesdale and lieutenant of the Marches of Scotland, married Mary, but before that he was visited by Mary at his fortress of Hermitage Castle. Bothwell in his position as Lord of the Marches was supposed to be keeping order, but actually was conniving in the raiding and bloodshed. For once he came off the worse in an encounter, and was stabbed and likely to die. Queen Mary rode from Jedburgh to see him and returned the same day, a distance of some sixty miles through wild country in cold and wet October weather. She became very ill, but when her illness had abated, she expressed the desire to return to Edinburgh via Berwick. The Governor of Berwick ordered all the soldiers to be on the walls with weapons and armour, and went out to the bound road with forty horsemen to greet her. Her retinue included Bothwell and they were accompanied by 500 horsemen. They went up to Halidon Hill, and while there, the great guns of Berwick were shot off all night in salute. This is a strange episode in the history of Berwick, and an involved story, but one which is worth the telling for it illustrates the ambivalence of the officers and governors of Berwick, who were presumably loyal servants of Queen Elizabeth, yet gave Mary Queen of Scots a signal honour when she 'looked on Berwick'.

Mary was forced to abdicate in favour of her son in 1567. As is well known, she was imprisoned and eventually, on the orders of Elizabeth, Mary was put on trial in 1587 and was convicted of plotting to harm the life of Elizabeth. She was forty-four when she was beheaded, the Dean of Peterborough calling out 'So perish all the Queen's enemies'.

Mary's son was twenty at the time of the execution, and as James VI of Scotland he had been on the throne since 1567 when he was only thirteen months old. Now everything was in place for him to succeed to the English throne, for on Elizabeth's death, he would be her rightful successor. Queen Elizabeth, however, was very much alive and would be for another sixteen years. She wanted the Borders brought under control and so she had, some years before, appointed a 'hard man' to the Captaincy of Berwick and Warden of the East March, one Henry Carey (Lord Hunsdon). In 1586, James VI and Elizabeth of England agreed a pact to keep the peace, and James was given a subsidy of £4,000 a year to help his straitened circumstances – this pact was drawn up in the Berwick Toll-booth on James's birthday, 27 June, and the money was to be paid from Berwick. It would appear that the money was

A peaceful re-enactment by Border Reivers at Norham Castle. As late as the seventeenth century, reivers were active, and Robert Carey who took the news of Elizabeth I's death to James VI of Scotland in 1603 gave orders to his deputies to keep the frontier quiet at this time. This was because of a widespread belief that when a monarch died the laws of the land were suspended until a new ruler was appointed. Carey's strictures were ignored, for burning and looting followed in the so-called 'ill week'.

frittered away, for his outlook was that money existed to be spent, in sharp contrast to Elizabeth, who always liked her books to be on the credit side. Elizabeth thought the money was well spent though, for James had been urged by some of his nobles to go to war against Elizabeth to revenge his mother's execution. In fact, the very next year the King was supposed to have ordered scaling ladders and engines to be gathered for a surprise attack on Berwick. This came to nothing, possibly because the King knew his subsidy from Elizabeth would immediately cease on such action.

One of the Queen's loyal servants, who would have liked some of the money which passed to James through Berwick, was Lord Hunsdon. He, as captain of the town, was constantly complaining about not being paid. Presumably he must have had some income, perhaps from the perks of his office, official or otherwise, but his salary always seemed to be in arrears. Another badly paid servant of the Queen was Rowland Johnson, who was overseer of the

The original stocks at the side of the Guild Hall in 1903. The gentleman is standing on the bottom step, which is a piece of carved masonry from the previous guild hall which had become dangerously ruinous in 1749. A guild hall has been on this site since the days of Alexander III.

works of the new walls (and also of a pier which was built at this time), who had not had an increase in pay for twenty years. The pier was built to improve the entrance at the harbour mouth, for ships were finding it increasingly difficult to navigate through the narrow entrance.

Another resident who would have been less than happy about his conditions, was one named Ayre, who was to be interrogated by the captains of the town regarding some seditious pamphlets which had been found. He was to be put on the rack, thumbscrews applied, and if this did not produce the 'truth', he was to have his feet put in the stocks wearing a pair of new shoes, which would then be set alight!

Other people were frightened of fire, for James VI had an obsession with witchcraft and witches, and any judged guilty of witchcraft were burnt alive, and before meeting their death subjected to hideous torture. James wrote a treatise, *Daemonologie*, an attack on those sceptical of witchcraft, and Berwick received a request from him to hand over a Scottish witch, who was thought to be in Berwick. A few years later, we find that the wife of a garrison man, Richard Swinbourne, had been in negotiations with three Berwick witches to do harm to her husband. When nothing happened to Richard, it was suggested it had to be a male witch (warlock) who would do the necessary evil thing. No record is known as to what happened to the witches, or Mrs Swinbourne who had wished to be rid of her husband, but their ends would not have been pleasant.

A meeting of over 100 witches at North Berwick Kirk was discovered to have been plotting the destruction of King James, who to be fair, was not inclined to believe the story. Francis, Earl of Bothwell, a cousin of the King, was implicated, and this would imply the witch hunt was political. Whether political or not, many were burned alive and when one claimed she was pregnant, physicians were ordered to examine her and if she was not, then 'to the fire with her and disembowel her publicly'.

The Devil was supposed to have addressed the witches' congregation and he was described so: 'His face was terrible, his nose was like the beak of an eagle, great burnin een, his hands and legs was hairy with claws upon his hands and he spoke with a rough deep voice'. Sounds remarkably like some Church of Scotland ministers of my childhood!

Living in a violent society such as this, it is no wonder many took to smoking tobacco, perhaps to calm their nerves, and it comes as no surprise that James wrote another treatise

For many years this RAC sign was on the pillar of the railway bridge, where Shielfield Terrace joins the old A1 in Tweedmouth.

entitled *Counterblast to Tobacco*. In it he compared smoking to excessive drinking – 'a custom loathsome to the eye, hateful to the nose, harmful to the brain, dangerous to the lungs,' and it must be said his perceptive writings were 360 years before their time.

The Border country was in ferment as usual, with feuds and raiding continuing – the Borders being the most unquiet place in England in 1603. Scott of Buccleuch and Kerr of Cessford, Wardens of the Middle March, were called to Berwick to account for their sins and omissions. Buccleuch had made a daring raid on Carlisle Castle to free Kinmont Willie, a noted freebooter. When asked by Queen Elizabeth how he dared do such a deed, Buccleuch replied, 'What is there a man dared not do?' which greatly impressed Elizabeth.

But time was running out for Elizabeth, for she was ill. Sir John Carey, the second son of Lord Hunsdon, was Governor of Berwick, Elizabeth having appointed him early in her reign. Robert Carey, another of Hunsdon's sons, had posted horses along the Great North Road, to be ready for a headlong ride to take the news to James VI of Scotland when Elizabeth died. On her death, Lady Scrope a lady in waiting, took a sapphire ring from the late Queen's finger and dropped it through a window to Robert Carey, her brother; this was to be proof that Elizabeth was dead and James was now King of England as well as of Scotland. Carey arrived in Edinburgh on the third day after a horrendous ride, having been thrown from his horse near Norham and suffering a severe head wound. He had covered 400 miles in 60 hours. As he crossed the Border he had word sent to his brother John in Berwick, so that Berwick received the news of Elizabeth's death before Edinburgh and King James.

Robert was anxious to be the first to greet James as King of England, for as Warden of the Middle March under his brother, he knew that with the merging of the two nations his job might disappear. Robert hoped for future favours from the King and he would not be disappointed. To be fair, Robert Carey had been one of Elizabeth's most influential and colourful courtiers, and probably deserved to be favoured. It was almost as if he had been in training for the ride north for most of his life. In 1589 he walked from London to Berwick in the record time of twelve days, winning in the process a substantial bet of £2,000. When it came to his momentous ride north he would therefore have been very familiar with the route.

CHAPTER 5
Stuarts and Puritans

A journey in the opposite direction was started by King James VI and I on 4 April 1603. He left Edinburgh, whose citizens seemed genuinely sorry to see him go, and the next day he arrived in Berwick. James had already been the recipient of a very flowery letter of loyalty from the Mayor of Berwick on behalf of the Corporation and inhabitants, and they obviously wanted to give the new King a warm welcome. It would appear from some accounts that someone in Berwick had knowledge of pyrotechnics, for when James arrived at the outskirts, the view was obscured by smoke which miraculously cleared to reveal 'an enchanted castle and the entrance to his new kingdom'. The more prosaic explanation is that the garrison had, in their exuberance, been firing all their guns in a royal salute. Such a magnificent 'peal of ordnance' had never before been known, so the smoke would be tremendous and the wind coming from an easterly direction would drift the smoke along the battlements.

However, it would make a good impression on the King and his large retinue of some 500 English and Scottish attendants. A welcoming speech was delivered and a church service followed, whereupon he went to the Palace 'amid the general rejoicing of the people'. He spent the night in Berwick, and walked on the walls the next day, even firing one of the guns, which was thought to be 'right kingly'. Leaving Berwick by the somewhat ramshackle wooden bridge, he was said to be unnerved by his passage across the bridge and asked plaintively, 'Is there never a man in Berwick that can boo stanes [bend or work stones] to build a brig over Berwick stream?'

The King knighted Mr William Selbie, Gentleman Porter of Berwick, on his arrival and Sir Ralph Grey on his departure. It is said he dubbed 237 knights on his way south from Scotland, and that the going rate for this honour was £1,000 to £2,000 (cash down)!

One of the first measures he took was to declare that the English-Scottish Borders should henceforth be known as the 'Middle Shires', and he was to be known as King of Great Britain, France and Ireland. He appointed George Home (third son of Alexander Home of Manderston) as Governor of Berwick and also of the East Marches. Subsequently Home was made Earl of Dunbar and Knight of the Garter. The Earl of Dunbar, along with Sir William Cranston on the Scottish side, began to clear up the mess which 300 years of war and raiding had left. A commission of justiciary was established as well as a type of police force, and it swung into action with a vengeance. The Earl of Dunbar hanged more than 140 of the most powerful thieves in all the Borders. His methods do not bear close scrutiny, for he hanged them first, then gave them a trial. This rough treatment became well known as 'Jeddart justice'. Some Border riding families were dispossessed and deported, some like Scott of Buccleuch took 2,000 of his followers to the Low Countries to fight as mercenaries, and not unnaturally the other inhabitants of the Borders were 'fully reduced to obedience', when they saw how merciless the new guardians of the Border could be. All this had a dramatic effect on

Berwick, for whereas before, it was the key to Scotland and England's strongest fortress town, rivalling any stronghold in Europe, now it was redundant.

The garrison in Berwick was drastically reduced to 100 soldiers and the guns were ordered to be sent to the Tower of London. Munitions and guns were brought from Scotland to Berwick to be shipped to London, one ship taking the ordnance being named the *Princess Elizabeth*. The quayside would have been busy, but really it was a winding-down operation for Berwick. The castle which in 1603 was granted to George Home, Earl of Dunbar, lost its garrison; thereupon the Earl commissioned Sir James Murray (James VI's last master of works) to design a colossal house, to be sited within the castle bounds. This work must have been well advanced and fairly complete when in 1611, Dunbar died suddenly and work ceased on his palace. Subsequently, much of the stone and wooden panelling was used in the building of the parish church (Holy Trinity). In the church today there is a chest with ornately carved panels, said to have been made with panelling from the castle. A man's portrait on the side is thought to show the Earl of Dunbar in profile.

By 1610 peace had been restored in the Borders and at last, it was worthwhile for people with land to think about developing and planning ahead. The plundering, raiding, and cattle rustling had

James I of England and VI of Scotland.

This chest in the parish church is made of panels carved by a Dutch master wood carver. The panels were removed from the Palace in Berwick Castle and the likeness on the left is thought to be that of the Earl of Dunbar, who commissioned the building of the Palace.

vanished and with their disappearance, a more settled way of life was possible. The great abbeys of the Borders were now of no importance; many had been destroyed and the monks who had continued living in parts of the monastic buildings gradually disappeared, not being allowed to recruit new members.

Even foreign affairs took a turn for the better, for after two decades of war, England made peace with Spain. However, trouble with the Spaniards continued despite the peace treaty, for in 1627 the Mayor of Berwick requested military assistance. It had been reported that the Spanish fleet was likely to come into Berwick or Holy Island after making a raid at Caithness. More troubles were reported concerning the piratical exploits of the 'Dunkirkers' – freebooters who sailed under the flag of Spain from the port of Dunkirk. It was a real enough threat, for they terrorized the mariners of the eastern coast of England. One of the Dunkirkers' ships was built as a galley, with thirty-two oars manned by slaves and carrying sixteen guns. At the end of the sixteenth century the governor of Berwick had been Peregrine Bertie, Lord Willoughby, and he had been so concerned about the activities of the Dunkirkers that he ordered a ship to be built of 140 tons with sixteen guns, to carry 100 fully armed men. The Berwick Mayor and Corporation objected to the expense, but the ship was built, presumably in Berwick. Willoughby was committed to attacking a Dunkirker which had taken as prize a ship laden with provisions of wheat and beans bound for Berwick. It was in the Firth of Forth, but Willoughby while waiting on board his ship for a favourable wind to sail north, caught a chill and subsequently died. Interestingly Willoughby had appointed his cousin John Guevara as Deputy Warden of the East March. Guevara was the Protestant grandson of a Spanish mercenary and had legal skills and a knowledge of martial law, which attributes had been of great advantage to Willoughby.

James's reign saw the decline of the British navy, for he was uninterested in military things. Perhaps if his great supporter and friend the Earl of Dunbar had lived, James would have been a wiser ruler. Nevertheless, he was responsible for bringing a measure of peace to the Borders, and when he made a visit to Scotland in 1617 he was warmly welcomed when he broke his journey in Berwick. He was presented with a 'propine' by the Mayor and Council, which really meant they had a night carousing and toasting the King's health. The next day, no doubt, he would inspect the work in progress on the stone bridge over the Tweed, which was commenced in 1611 after the fall of the wooden bridge in 1608. The Burgh was indebted to the Earl of Dunbar who secured the grant to commence building the bridge, and if the Earl had lived, no doubt he would have raised the funds necessary to build a new church, which was badly needed. Also to the credit of James, was his instigation of a new translation of the Bible which took fifty men of letters six years to produce. The Bible we know today as the King James Authorized Version is monumental in the beauty of the words chosen and its use of the English language.

James VI of Scotland and I of England died in 1625 aged fifty-eight, having ruled as a king for fifty-seven years. He was succeeded by his son Charles I, aged twenty-five, who would be notable for being tried for treason and beheaded after a twenty-four-year reign. In 1633 Charles, while on a journey to Edinburgh, stopped off at Berwick for ten days, staying at His Majesty's Palace in Berwick. Much fawning by the town's fathers ensued before he and his retinue numbering more than 600 set off for Edinburgh, where he was to be crowned King of

Scotland. The Earl of Home's men were dressed in green satin doublets and white dimity scarves (a sort of padded waistcoat with woven corded cotton scarves). It was not long before Charles aroused anger in his Scottish subjects by trying to introduce new aspects of religious observance, including the imposition of bishops, which his Scottish subjects thought smacked of 'popery'. Thus was the Covenanting movement forged, which also had sympathizers in England. As the Duke of Northumberland pointed out when the King threatened to use force to subdue the Scots, 'a greater part of any English army would be more likely to join with the Scots than to draw their swords for the King.'

Berwick was inclined to favour the Covenanters' cause, although the Mayor denied that Berwick harboured any in the town, saying any semblance of military activity by the townspeople was purely because they were ready to defend themselves against any approaching armies.

Nevertheless 600 soldiers of the King under Lord Essex did take over Berwick in 1639, having entered the town by the newly built bridge. This, no doubt, was in response to the taking by the Covenanters of the castles of Edinburgh, Stirling and Dumbarton. The King's soldiers 'found no enemies except what was constant to this place [Berwick] – snow, hail and violent northern winds.'

When the main part of the English army, numbering some 20,000, arrived with King Charles, their camp was set up four miles west of Berwick on the south side of the Tweed (opposite Paxton House) at Yarrow Haugh. Until a pavilion was erected for Charles he 'lodged' in Berwick. The conditions in the camp as well as in Berwick were becoming intolerable, and food was extremely scarce, the soldiers in Berwick 'snatching people's dinners from them'. Smallpox and vermin were rife, and the shelter afforded the camp soldiers was turf walls with gorse or whin bushes laid on top for a roof. It was no wonder that desertion was a common occurrence and Charles, faced with a strong Covenanting army under General Leslie, decided to yield and a truce was declared, subsequently to be known as the Pacification

Berwick Old Bridge was built on medieval lines, although building was commenced in 1611. With fifteen arches and a total length of 1164ft, its highest arch is the second arch from Berwick, this to allow headroom for the masts of sailing ships.

of Berwick. The King signed but probably with fingers crossed, for he had no intention of being thwarted in his plans. So the First Bishops' War ended. The Second Bishops' War would follow just a year later, when the Covenanters led by General Leslie took Newcastle and yet again another truce was signed. These wars would carry on for another ten years, and would merge into the Civil Wars. In the beginning Scotland was fighting the battle for theological reasons, and this was aiding the English Parliamentarians in their political fight for freedom against King Charles. The King believed he had absolute power, which was

Cowport, c. 1902. The gentleman on the right has just filled two watering cans from a fountain on the wall, immediately behind him.

adverse to the liberty of the individual, so that for instance dissenters could be imprisoned for life, after having their ears cut off – not much charity there! Religious fanaticism continued for another forty years, tearing the country apart and destroying lives and national wealth, and during that period Berwick suffered probably more than most towns.

As regards the town's fortifications, the wall which had been built in the fourteenth century along the top of the high bank of the river, from the back of the present Tweed Street to Megs Mount, was strengthened and probably heightened. (Today there is a path leading from Castle Vale Park which follows this wall.) A drawbridge was made at the Cowport and new gates were made for the northern entrances.

In 1642 the Mayor of Berwick turned down flat a request by the King to allow a recruiting drive for his army – the reply was unequivocal: 'There will be no beating of a drum for raising soldiers.' A confessed Papist was ordered out of town, and the

Plan of Charles I's camp in 1639, in the area between Longridge and Paxton, known as The Birks or sometimes Yarrow Haugh.

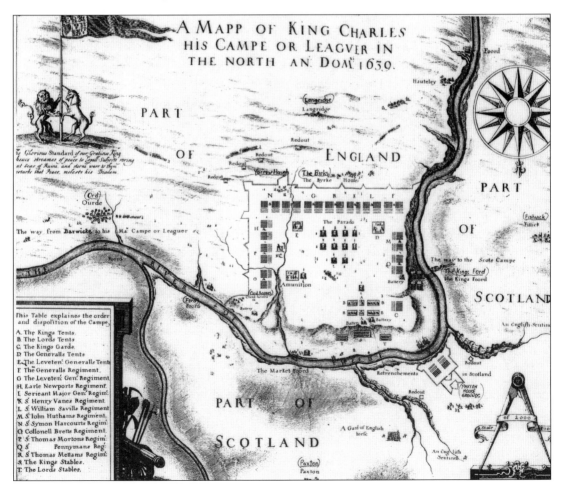

burgesses had to report with their best guns and stand nightly watch. Threats by the Cavaliers were met with steely disdain. These threats were followed by wheedling requests that the sentries might be removed from the bridge, presumably to allow the Royalists to take over Berwick. To aid the independence of Berwick, the commander of the Parliamentarians' fleet stationed a warship in the bay, and the town was garrisoned by Scottish troops sympathetic to the English Parliamentarians. A large Scottish army which supported the anti-royalists did yeoman service in England, having crossed the Tweed when frozen over in the winter of 1643/44. Charles finally surrendered to them at Newark in 1646, and this eventually led to his execution in 1649.

Now Oliver Cromwell was Lord Protector of the Commonwealth of England and his former allies, the Scots, became his enemies, for they had proclaimed Charles I's son as King Charles II. In 1648 the Cavaliers, numbering 1,000 foot soldiers and 800 horse, took Berwick over and, imposing themselves on the residents, shortly had them in dire straits as they were not able to provide for themselves and the Royalists. The Cavaliers were evacuated and the Scots took over, and they in turn gave up possession when Cromwell appeared with a regiment of foot and a regiment of horse. Now conditions got worse, with citizens having to give up their houses to accommodate soldiers and poorer residents having to pawn their possessions to survive.

Colonel George Fenwick now became the Governor of Berwick, which had become a northern centre of the Civil War. He was a great friend of the Protector (Cromwell), and he was able to secure provisions in good quantity, for the betterment of conditions of both the soldiers and the citizens. He also obtained twelve mounted brass guns from the Tower of London for defence of the town, as well as other guns from castles at Wallingford and Pontefract. As the summer of 1650 wore on, more ships were loaded with supplies to be brought to Berwick including 400,000lb of biscuits, 18 tons of cheese, (two types – Cheshire and Suffolk, the latter, at £28 per ton, being £5 a ton cheaper than Cheshire), oats and wheat in great quantity. Tents, hand mills, boots, shoes, cloaks, kettles were to be sent – in short, everything to equip and maintain an army on the march, for all this preparation would culminate in the Battle of Dunbar, when Cromwell would decisively defeat the Scottish army. The Scots, led by General Leslie, had superior numbers and despite all Cromwell's preparations, the ships with the provisions arrived late at Berwick and had to sail further north, but by then Cromwell's army was starving, and the battle was only won through the fatal intervention of the Scottish religious leaders. They had urged Leslie to abandon his strong position, assuring him that God had guaranteed his assistance, but God let them down, for 3,000 Scots were killed and 6,000 taken prisoner.

The Scots taken prisoner were brought to Berwick before being taken to Newcastle. At Berwick they were grateful to the Governor who organised food rations for them – 'for one day three biskits and a pottle of pease' (pot of pease pudding). This ration they said, was more than their own officers gave them for three days. The old adage about an army marching on its stomach would seem applicable here.

A tradition lingers that Cromwell stayed in the Black Bull Inn (Silver Street) when he passed through Berwick in 1650, and he may well have done, but normally he encamped at Mordington, four miles north west of Berwick. Berwick was fortunate in that during the Civil

Wars, while there certainly was deprivation, there was no assault on the town by armies. Indeed, the present-day parish church was being built at this time, and tradition has it that Cromwell inspected the works, personally vetoing plans for a tower – such a decoration being frowned on by the Puritans.

No doubt the conduct of one of Cromwell's troopers would have been frowned on, had it been known of at the time of the Battle of Dunbar. It was eight years later that the Dunbar Kirk Session records disclose that 'Margaret Home was rebuked for her fall in fornication with John Bahill, trooper in General Cromwell's regiment in 1651'. She was fined £3 Scots. (Until Union in 1707, the pound Scots was worth a twelfth of a pound sterling, or 1s 8d.)

The Puritans must, however, have indulged in some innocent leisure, for a piece of ground was granted by the town so that the Governor and the garrison could have a bowling green. Likewise the Governor's House and other houses in the Palace were given over to them to use as they wished. Soldiers of the garrison offered to clear away huge mountains of dung which had accumulated in the Parade, Eastern Lane, and the Newgate, but they required payment. £12 cleared the Parade and £4 Eastern Lane, but the unfortunate Newgate was left uncleared for the Guild could not afford the payment. This was not a new problem, however, as the records for 100 years before (and continuing for more than a 100 years after) make reference to 'dounghells befor ther dors, both wenter and somer which is a shameful sight in the King's town and very noysome' (vexatious). This problem is not to be wondered at, for hundreds of cattle and horses would be quartered in the town, and every day they would be led out to the pastures surrounding the

This portrait of a Puritan lady, painted in 1638, is in the Borough Museum, and is part of the collection gifted by Sir William Burrell.

Bowling is a serious business, and it may be bad for the back!

In the barracks, the Clock Block on the left houses the Berwick Borough Museum and Art Gallery. There is a fascinating exhibition, 'A Window on Berwick', and also other displays and many items and paintings from the Burrell collection.

town. It is not surprising therefore that outbreaks of plague kept recurring, and presaging that in London in 1665. In this year Berwick had taken precautions against the plague; travellers had to provide certificates of safety and boats had to lie in the river for six weeks if they came from suspect places. Berwick did however suffer a Great Fire in 1659, mirroring London's fire of 1666. All these disasters seemed to have a lowering effect on the general morale, and portents of disaster were seized on with avidity. It was reported nationally that after the Great Fire of London, sentries in Berwick had seen 'the likeness of abundance of ships in the air'. Perhaps a local Nostradamus was at work, foretelling the air attacks on Berwick in the Second World War!

Oliver Cromwell died in 1658, and was succeeded by his son Richard, who ruled for one year, and then in 1660 the monarchy was restored in the person of Charles II – the Merry Monarch. This was thanks to the efforts of General Monk who had fought for Cromwell at the Battle of Dunbar, and was made Governor of Scotland. Monk, seeing the confusion caused by the death of Cromwell, negotiated with Charles in exile in France, and brought him back to England and set him on the throne. During these quick-fire changes of ruler, Berwick's Mayor and Burgesses never missed an opportunity to rejoice 'with all sorts of wine that could be had', and bonfires which blazed in the market place while loyal messages were sent to every new incumbent of the throne.

Berwick Castle must have been pretty well dismantled by this time for in 1666, the Governor obtained the two 'Gate Steads' (pillars) of the Castle. These were to be erected as an ornament to a house he was about to build on the bridge for the Watch. Permission was granted, but only on condition that in the structure there would be a room large enough to seat the local dignitaries when they were waiting to greet any 'great person' coming to the town. This gatehouse can be seen in old engravings at the north end of the bridge, and it must have been a substantial building when it was removed in 1825.

In the early 1680s Charles II decided to tighten the screws on boroughs such as Berwick, who had not looked unfavourably on Cromwell. To do this and to have a more subservient Parliament, he needed to have representatives in the various towns who would support his decisions. In the case of Berwick, the Charter, which conferred great privileges on the town, was withdrawn. A dispute regarding the younger son of a freeman living in London who was refused permission by the Guild to be admitted as a freeman, was used as the excuse for the removal of the Charter. A deputation from the town had to travel to London to surrender the Charter, which took them twelve days. This somewhat protracted journey and a delay in being received by the King had unfortunate consequences, for the King took ill and died. Now the deputation had to await the favour of the new King James II (VII of Scotland). The new King was even less well disposed to his subjects from Berwick, and told them if they wanted the privilege of a new charter, they would have to 'bring in more honest men to the town'. This was achieved by the King sacking most of Berwick's governing body, including the Mayor, and appointing his own men in their place. The new Mayor was Ferdinando Forster and Forster's ceremonial halberts, bearing his initials, can be seen today in the Mayor's parlour in the Guild Hall.

James II, a Catholic, was a tyrant who persecuted the Covenanters and placed Catholics in positions of authority. Any who opposed him suffered from dreadful acts of revenge. His Chief

A section of Buck's engraving of 1745 shows the White Wall with a fully extended arm built into the river from the Water Tower at the base of the castle mound.

Justice, Jeffreys, earned notoriety at this time by hanging 350 rebels in his circuit through Dorset and Somerset (the 'Bloody Assizes') and sending hundreds into slavery. Women were burned, scourged or sent to the block for slight transgressions.

It must have been with a great sense of relief, therefore, that Berwick learned of the flight of James II and VII to France, driven away by the fear of a popular uprising. Even the Tories who had supported the Crown could not continue to support James in his tyrannical behaviour. A hypocrite as well as a tyrant, he had numerous plain-looking mistresses and these were explained away later as being penances imposed by his priests! Now, hopes in Berwick in 1689 were pinned to James II's successor to the throne, William III, a Dutchman, who had married his cousin Mary, daughter of James II. All the spurious councillors who had ruled Berwick for two years were turned out of office; the old council was brought back and the royal charter was restored. The bells rang, bonfires blazed and quantities of wine were consumed in the celebrations.

The accession of William III (of Orange) and his wife Mary as joint sovereigns was not universally welcomed in Scotland where the Jacobites (loyal to James II and VII of Scotland) were opposed to the Protestants. The Scottish Highlands were anything but settled, and so Berwick continued to be a garrison town, but the inhabitants were rebellious about soldiers being billeted on them. A petition was raised to have proper accommodation made available to the troops in the shape of purpose-built barracks. This would relieve the pressure on the town's inns and private householders, and an added bonus would be the confining of unruly and thieving soldiers to the barracks at night.

With William and Mary both dead, the crown of the realm was placed on the head of James II and VII's second daughter, Anne, in 1702. She ruled for twelve years, during which time the Act of Union was accomplished between England and Scotland in 1707. During her reign, the country was virtually governed by the Duke of Marlborough and his wife. Marlborough, an ancestor of Sir Winston Churchill, drove the Spanish from the Netherlands and defeated the French at Blenheim and Ramillies, and eventually the fortifications at the port of Dunkirk were demolished when France acknowledged defeat. Dunkirk was the base for the privateers who had so harassed the mariners and fishermen of Eastern England that they could not venture out of their ports. In the Berwick records, numerous references are made to the 'Dunkirkers' and the threat they posed, so it is no wonder we find the Town Clerk of Berwick, aided by the Master of the Grammar School, writing flowery and obsequious letters of loyalty to the Queen.

CHAPTER 6
Hanoverians to the Present

The death of Queen Anne in 1714 resulted in the accession to the British throne of the first of the Hanoverians, George I. George, as Prince Ruler of Hanover in Germany, had co-operated with Marlborough in opposing Louis XIV's plans for the conquest of Europe. Much more importantly, however, George's mother was the grand-daughter of James I of England, hence his right of succession. In Berwick as is to be expected, the barrel was rolled out when George I was crowned. An entertainment was held, the magistrates inviting their cronies to the celebration, and in addition each member of the Guild received 2s for drink money. Later in the century, the profligacy of the Corporation in such matters would result in serious financial problems for Berwick.

In 1715, an alarm of serious proportions jolted Berwick out of its celebratory mood, when the Jacobite adherents surfaced once more, to champion the cause of the 'Old Pretender', son of James II (VII of Scotland). The Catholic gentry rose in Northumberland under the young Lord Derwentwater and Mr Forster of Bamburgh, but it was to no avail, and Derwentwater lost his head to the axe at Tower Hill in 1716. His estates, which included the Manor of Scremerston, were forfeited and the revenues of Scremerston and estates in Cumbria were allotted to Greenwich Hospital, London, which was founded for the care of elderly and disabled sailors. Greenwich Hospital still holds many farms and estates in the Berwick area, as well as the mineral rights to the coal deposits in the Scremerston mines.

A drastic decision was taken in Berwick, that some houses in Castlegate should be demolished, and levelled to the ground. This was to afford the guns on the Middle Mount (now Cumberland Bastion), a clear field of fire in case the Jacobite forces attacked the town. Ten companies of volunteers, forty men in each company, were ordered to be at the ready, under the captaincy of the Mayor and Justices of the town, and for three months till the

Scremerston coal mine, c. 1900.

Lindisfarne Castle, owned by the National Trust. It was built during the reign of Henry VIII with stone robbed from the Priory. This contrasts with Berwick where stone from the Castle was used in the building of the parish church.

middle of December 1715, strict watch was kept. Down the coast, Holy Island Castle was actually taken on behalf of the Pretender, but the story has an element of a Ruritanian farce about it. Only two men (out of a garrison of seven) were holding the castle, and one Samuel Phillipson acted as, or was, a barber! Two brothers by the name of Errington, who had a trader ship, came to Holy Island, and Lancelot Errington obtained admission to the castle saying he wanted his beard shaven. He drew out his pistol and declared the castle was his in the name of the Pretender, thrusting the two defenders out into the cold. The next day, some soldiers from the Berwick garrison rescued the castle with no great trouble, and the Erringtons were committed to the gaol in the Old Tolbooth.

To the right of the Scots Gate are the Cockle Steps, surmounted by the original archway from the old gate. The arch is thought to have been resited to the steps when the old gate was widened in 1815. Cope would have clattered under the original arch when fleeing on his horse from the defeat at Prestonpans in 1745.

Scots Gate, Berwick.

Subsequently with the help of some local men, including one Freeman of the Borough, they escaped along with other prisoners by pulling up the flagstones at the doorway of the gaol and crawling under the door. Thirty-four years later, the tolbooth fell down and perhaps this would explain how the prisoners could make such an easy escape.

In 1745, the alarums and excursions were all repeated, due to the appearance on the scene of the Young Pretender, grandson of James II (VII of Scotland). Bonnie Prince Charlie, who had come from the exiled Stuart court in Rome, raised his standard at Glenfinnan near Fort William. He brought his forces to Edinburgh, which fell without resistance, the Government officials fleeing to the safety of Berwick. This sudden influx of panic-stricken civil servants would no doubt have alarmed the Berwick authorities who wrote for and obtained permission to form companies of volunteers and to take up arms. Their first sight of a soldier at the gates was, however, no attacking Highlander, but Lieutenant-General Sir John Cope, commander of the Government forces, who had been soundly defeated at Prestonpans, some 45 miles north-west of Berwick. He demanded admission into Berwick in the King's name, and on being asked who he was, he uttered one word 'Cope'. The drawbridge was lowered, the gates opened, and the General who had left his troops behind to gallop to safety, entered the Main Guard. He was subsequently court-martialled and died in 1760, but his name lives on in the mocking Scottish song, 'Heigh! Johnnie Cope are ye waken yet?', for it was said he was not ready when the Highlanders attacked. Berwick then became a refuge for soldiers fleeing from the rout, including many wounded who were cared for, all of this adding to the fear of the townspeople and the Corporation, who expected Berwick to be attacked very soon. Much to their relief, however, Prince Charlie divided his forces on his march south, one column crossing the Tweed at Kelso, meeting up with the other column at Carlisle, before advancing as far as Derby. Later, thousands of troops including Dutch and Flemish soldiers would march through Berwick on their way north, where they would, under the Duke of Cumberland, decisively beat the Highlanders at the Battle of Culloden.

The Jacobite cause was finished, for even English Catholic supporters of the Stuart dynasty, who were averse to the ruling House of Hanover, had not risen to support Prince Charles when he appealed for help. Henceforth, the Highlands would be brought under the same strict control as had the Border Country more than 100 years before.

Berwick Town Hall and steeple, built in the 1750s. Joseph Dodds, a local freeman, is credited with its architectural design, but Samuel and John Worrall of London had submitted plans and were paid £31 10s. It has a striking resemblance to a London church (St Giles in the Fields) which was built in the style of Wren, by Henry Flitcroft. It is possible that Dodds used the original London plans which might explain the remarkable similarity.

Two years after the aborted efforts of the Young Pretender's bid for the crown, the mood in Berwick must have been more confident. The Guild began to consider a replacement building for the Tolbooth, which was in a bad state of repair. In 1749 the Tolbooth indeed did fall down, the bell steeple being in great decay, as was the gaol. Work began in 1750, and the imposing building with its 150ft high steeple was completed in seven years. The bells from the old Tolbooth were sent to London to be recast, and a clock with four faces in stone was fitted in the steeple.

In agriculture, improvements and innovations were taking place. Fields belonging to the Borough were enclosed, allowing rotation of crops, and manuring was improving the fertility of the soil. Some years previously Daniel Defoe, political commentator and author of *Robinson Crusoe* and *A Tour through Great Britain*, visited Berwick and recorded the improvement in agriculture in the area. He wrote about white clover (which is the sweetest type of pasture) abounding in the natural grass even on the highway sides and the ramparts of Berwick. A little beyond Berwick, he saw a field of lucerne (a clover-like fodder plant) which was superior to anything he had seen before. The barley was as fine and strong as could possibly grow, and turnip husbandry was well practised. Turnips had been introduced from Sweden and the local name for turnip, bagie, is derived from the Swedish turnip, rutabaga.

Defoe was also impressed with the salmon trade, which at that time was a valuable export. All Tweed-caught salmon should have been cured and pickled locally, but some found their way to Newcastle before being cured and sent to London. Defoe rather indignantly thought the salmon which he was familiar with in London, known as Newcastle salmon, should be called Berwick salmon. The burgesses of Berwick however, knew that there was little they could do, for many of the fishing stells were on the Tweedmouth and Spittal side of the river, which came under the jurisdiction of Durham. This was why there was always a clod of turf on the sixth pier (from the Berwick side) of the bridge, to mark the boundary between Berwick and North Durham. The coopers who made the barrels and containers for salmon were skilled craftsmen, and many moved to London to further their fortunes, and in 1796

Salmon fishermen working with traditional method of wear-shot netting at the Gardo fishing station (or stell). This is now the only station being worked in the estuary, from more than twenty working in the last century.

there were sixteen freemen working as coopers in the district of Southwark, London.

Later, the salmon trade would have a beneficial effect on the shipbuilding industry in Berwick, for the requirement of fast ships to transport fish from Berwick to London, led to the innovation of a sailing ship which was recognized as being revolutionary – the Berwick Smack.

In the mid-eighteenth century, the Guild gave permission to a non-freeman, Arthur Byram, to establish a shipbuilding yard, and it is thought that the original plan for the Berwick Smack emanated from him. In consequence of ships being built at Berwick, there was a demand for ropes, blocks, sails etc., and industries making these soon followed.

Berwick's defences were not being neglected though, for there were always wars in which Britain was involved. In the 1760s. during the time of the Seven Years' War, which involved almost the whole of Europe and when England supported Prussia, the Walls received significant attention. The walls from the present-day Ness Gate past Fishers fort to Coxon's Tower, and from there along the Quayside to Meg's Mount, were substantially reconstructed. A few years previously, the garrison magazine had been built to store gunpowder and munitions, and for safety the walls were strongly buttressed. Copper was used in the metal door and wooden plugs were used instead of nails, all to reduce the danger of explosion.

The French revolutionary wars and the Napoleonic Wars caused some alarm in Berwick, and when France declared war on

A passage exists under the walls, from the east end of the Quay Walls to the Shoregate. Over the centuries, owners of houses abutting the walls have blocked off parts for their own use. Here, the late Mr G. Herbert stands in the passage of No. 21, which was formerly the home of Thomas Sword Good.

This aquatint of 1822 shows the horse-drawn railway, which carried coal from Scremerston to the quay at Hallowstell, Spittal. The railway was first used for the transport of the quarried stone required for the building of the pier.

The garrison magazine built in 1749, showing how the barrels of gunpowder were stored in racks.

Britain in 1793, the fear of invasion was ever present. Nothing untoward happened, however, and apart from contributing £1,000 to the Government for the prosecution of the war, and making provision for widows and children of those killed in the battles, Berwick was peaceful.

In their deliberations on how to improve Berwick, the Guild began to think of building a new pier for better navigation to encourage the trade of the port. Work started in 1810, when stone from the cliffs just south east of Spittal were brought by a horse-drawn railway to the jetty at Hallowstell. Barges then took the huge blocks across the river where workmen laboured at interlocking them to make a strong storm-proof pier, 960 yards long. The pier was finally finished in 1821 and a lighthouse was erected some five years later.

When George IV succeeded to the British throne in 1820, he was the fourth consecutive Hanoverian George to reign over Britain, the four Georges covering a period of more than 100 years. Great was the anticipation therefore when George IV announced he would visit his Scottish subjects in 1822. Berwick had not had a royal visitor for centuries and perhaps the burgesses hoped he would stop off on his royal progress to Edinburgh, as had many sovereigns in the past. No doubt they would have liked him to admire their splendid new pier, and enjoy a bumper of wine with them in the evening. He did indeed see the pier, for his journey north was by royal yacht which anchored in Berwick Bay. The royal yacht was being towed by a paddle steamer which had exhausted its coal stocks, and Berwick's dignitaries responded with alacrity to the request for a supply of fuel. Sheldon the historian

For almost two hundred years, mariners approaching Berwick would have seen this view, with the Lions House and the Town Hall steeple prominent landmarks on the skyline.

This drawing by W. Wilson (c. 1850) of the temporary railway bridge is in the Borough Museum. The stone piers of the Royal Border Bridge designed by Robert Stephenson are shown in their completed state. When the temporary structure was completed in 1848, the navvies, numbering more than 2,500, were rewarded with mugs of ale.

dips his pen in acid regarding this episode when he writes thus: 'The Worshipful Mayor and the Treasurer having freighted a barge with the necessary fuel, stood out to the royal yacht; and having delivered their cargo were thanked and entertained with a cold collation by His Majesty. This was but poor reward for their energy and labour on his behalf. They lingered about the yacht, some vain ideas of knighthood glimmering in their minds, until the steamer getting under weigh, effectually dispelled their dreams of greatness. With a bad grace the representatives of the good old town returned to Berwick venting their spleen on the king's head in no very measured terms, who regardless of their disappointment steamed away to the Firth of Forth'. This undoubtedly would be a true account, for Sheldon was writing just twenty-six years after the event, although it must be said, he writes of the dignitaries' chagrin with a strong flavour of satisfaction, which is very human.

From George IV who did not visit Berwick and disappointed the dignitaries, to Queen Victoria who did visit Berwick and disappointed the citizens, is a jump of just twenty-eight years, but much had happened in that time. In 1825 the Stockton and Darlington railway line had opened, and from that time, steam transport whether by ship or by railway locomotive was

The Flying Scotsman *(no. 4486) in streamlined mode, approaching the south end of the Royal Border Bridge, the curvature of the bridge showing clearly. Over one million tons of soil were manhandled by navvies in creating the embankment on the Tweedmouth approach to the bridge.*

to have a transforming effect on people's lives. A railway line was opened in 1846 which linked Edinburgh and Berwick, and a year later Tweedmouth was linked to Newcastle. Obviously a bridge was needed to connect Tweedmouth and Berwick, but it would be a formidable undertaking, because of the height and length required to cross the River Tweed. In 1848 a temporary wooden bridge 1,200ft long and 140ft high was constructed. In itself this was something of a miracle, for it resembled the massive trestle bridges built in America, when the railways were being driven west, but that was some twenty-five years later. The first passenger train passed over this wooden viaduct in October 1848, and though work on the stone bridge was being facilitated by the wooden bridge, it is still remarkable that the bridge we know today was completed in three years.

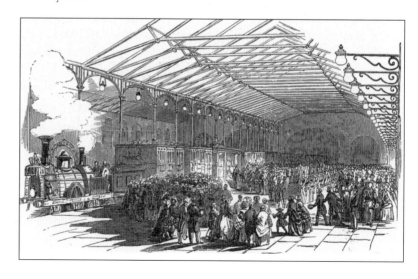

The Illustrated London News *published this woodcut in its issue of August 1850. The Mayor of Berwick can be seen presenting the loyal address to Queen Victoria.*

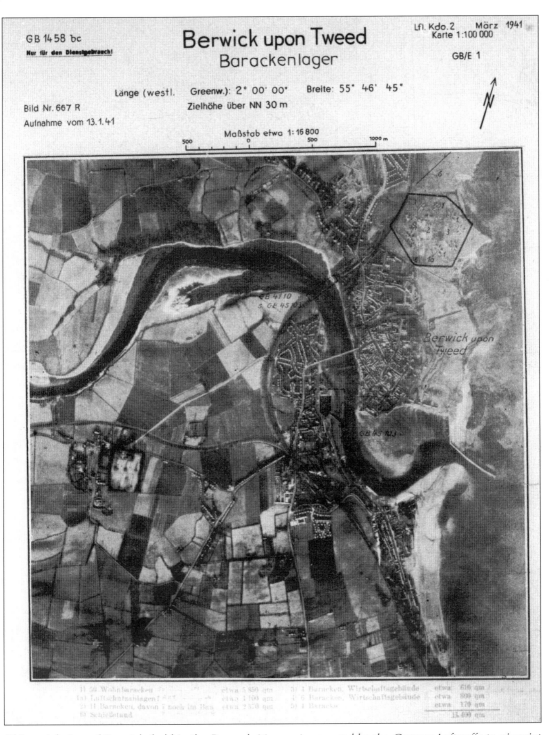

GB 1458 bc
Nur für den Dienstgebrauch!

Berwick upon Tweed
Barackenlager

Lfl. Kdo. 2   März 1941
Karte 1:100 000

GB/E 1

Länge (westl. Greenw.): 2° 00' 00"   Breite: 55° 46' 45"

Bild Nr. 667 R
Aufnahme vom 13.1.41

Zielhöhe über NN 30 m

Maßstab etwa 1:16 800

This aerial view of Berwick (held in the Borough Museum) was used by the German Luftwaffe to pinpoint prime targets for bombing during the Second World War. The targets included the Royal Border Bridge, Tweedmouth Docks, and the military installations in the area now occupied by the Holiday Centre.

Hence the great excitement when Queen Victoria and her consort Prince Albert arrived by royal train from the south on the official opening day in August 1850. After crossing the bridge the train stopped briefly at Berwick station, where the Queen named it the Royal Border Bridge, and after a stay of less than ten minutes, the royal train drew out of the station. All this was a great disappointment to the populace numbering some 12,000, who naturally hoped they were going to see something of a royal spectacle.

It would be a further seventy-eight years before Berwick saw another royal personage in the shape of the Prince of Wales opening the Royal Tweed Bridge in 1928, and what a disappointment he proved to be! Perhaps it is not to be wondered at, that when the Berwick bypass bridge was opened in 1983, no royal dignitary was asked to perform the ceremony, much to the annoyance of the *Tweeddale Press* at the time, who thought this was shameful!

It might be thought that, with the age of science and industrial innovation having taken over from the age of faith and slavish subjection to church, king and country, that wars would not affect Berwick ever again. This sadly was not the case, for the Kings Own Scottish Borderers (Volunteer Company) went to war in South Africa at the time of the Boer War. As Berwick Barracks was the depot for the KOSB from 1881 to 1964, the town saw men marching off to war in 1899, 1914 and 1939.

In the Second World War, Berwick was under enemy attack once more, this time from air action. By the end of the war twenty-five civilians had been killed by bombs, twenty-five houses had been demolished and 144 seriously damaged. Most of the damage and all the fatalities occurred in Spittal and Tweedmouth, although there were incendiary and machine gun attacks on Berwick. As in the days of siege warfare, food became scarce and although a rationing system theoretically ensured everybody got the same, there was a 'black market' where items in short supply could be exchanged for higher than the regulated prices. To guard against sea invasion, barbed wire defences and poles were erected on the beaches of Spittal and Berwick, anti-aircraft guns were placed on the Elizabethan Walls, and shore defence guns were mounted in concrete emplacements. At the same time, the old cannons on the ramparts were taken away to be melted down and reforged into modern weapons of war.

When peace came celebrations were muted, for many Berwickers in common with the nation as a whole, had lost loved ones. For the survivors the time of austerity carried on with rationing of some foods continuing until 1953.

One sad footnote to this long record of war and fatalities is that during the Falklands war in 1982 a Tweedmouth seaman, Paul Henry, serving on the stricken Royal Fleet Auxiliary ship, the *Sir Galahad*, sacrificed his own life to save that of a comrade. For this he was awarded the George Medal posthumously.

CHAPTER 7
Tweedmouth and Spittal

The area of Tweedmouth would have been known to the Romans, for there is evidence of a camp at Sunnyside. Subsequently, there was perhaps a settlement in Saxon times, which no doubt would suffer at the hands of the Danes. A religious house may have been established as far back as the seventh century, for an early church was dedicated to St Boisil (a Prior of Old Melrose), and he died in 661. It is thought that the Tweedmouth Feast originates from a religious celebration which took place around St Boisil's day, 18 July. Certainly St Boswells Fair was always opened on 18 July and St Boswells, 34 miles south west of Berwick, got its name from St Boisil who built a cell where the present St Boswells parish church stands. The Tweedmouth Feast grew into a great trading fair, which was well established in the thirteenth century, subsequently being curtailed at one point, at the request of the Berwick burgesses, when it became a threat to the Berwick traders' businesses.

Tweedmouth was looked on by successive English kings as a springboard for operations against Berwick and Scotland. Thus it was that King John of England began to fortify a castle in Tweedmouth in 1204, ostensibly to defend the ford over the Tweed, the point of entrance to the river being almost opposite his castle site. King William (the Lion, of Scotland) objected, as he deemed it a threat to his castle at Berwick. William sent a force across the river, who attacked the builders and razed the castle to the ground. John gave orders for the castle to be rebuilt, and again it was attacked and demolished. This might have continued for decades, but in 1209, a treaty was concluded at Norham between the two kings and an uneasy truce ensued. There may have been another tower in Tweedmouth, or even a castle, and the

Tweedmouth as represented in an aquatint of 1750. The river spreads to a shelving shore where the docks are now. No railway line cuts through the landscape, which shows many cultivated fields which are now under housing estates.

Tweedmouth parish church has a distinctive weather vane in the shape of a salmon, indicating the importance the salmon-fishing trade once had. In the background, the tall masts of a three-masted sailing ship can be seen.

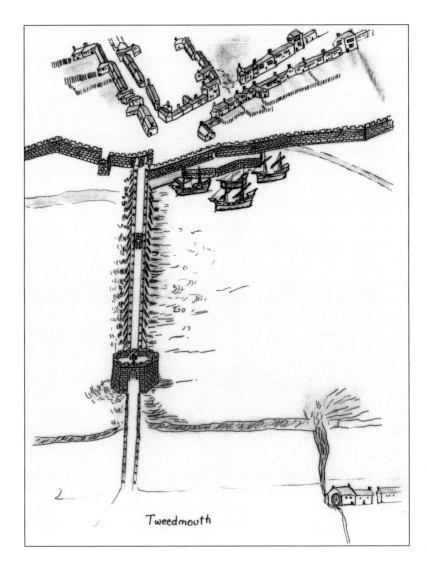

Tweedmouth

This map of 1570 shows the wooden bridge with a stone tower complete with a cannon on top, and a defensive wooden structure half-way over. This bridge was the one which so unnerved James VI on his journey south to be crowned James I of England.

present Tower Road and Mount Road would suggest it was situated in this area. Francis Cowe, the eminent Berwick historian, has made a convincing case for a castle on the site of Knowe Head, but to date, there have been no excavations, and if it was of the motte and bailey type, then there would be little to find.

In 1278 a dispute between Alexander III of Scotland and the Bishop of Durham, regarding the boundaries of England and Scotland in the Eastern Marches, resulted in a conference at Tweedmouth. The Scottish commissioners quartered in Berwick, while the English representatives lodged in Tweedmouth. Presumably they did meet for their discussions (perhaps in the triangular area in the West End of Tweedmouth where there is a Parliament Close) and although an agreement was eventually concluded, it happened some time after these deliberations.

In 1604, James VI (Scotland) and I (England) granted the Manor of Tweedmouth and Spittal to his great favourite the Earl of Dunbar. The Earl (formerly Lord Home of Berwick, third son of Alexander Home of Manderston), had, as Governor of Berwick and of the East Marches, pacified the Borders, gained a favourable royal charter for Berwick, and had also obtained the grant to build the present bridge over the Tweed. He was thus a worthy recipient of his King's favours. Subsequently, after his death, the Manor of Tweedmouth and Spittal descended to his son-in-law, the Earl of Suffolk, who in 1657 sold it to the Berwick Corporation for £570 – the best bargain Berwick ever made! Perhaps this is why even today, one can detect a certain reservation on the part of the older residents of Spittal and Tweedmouth regarding Berwick, for they may think their forebears' rights were sold too cheaply!

In any case, the townships of Tweedmouth and Spittal were swallowed up completely in 1835. Until that time, they had existed as separate and distinct entities as regards administrative matters. In 1831, a proposal had been put forward that they be incorporated into a newly defined and enlarged Borough of Berwick, this most probably because Berwick was declining and they were expanding. Trade was increasing in both Tweedmouth and Spittal, and the latter was also becoming recognized as a sea-bathing place and spa. At this time on the Berwick side of the river, only smacks and small brigs with a capacity of less than 200 tons could be loaded from the quays, due to the river bed being rocky and incapable of being deepened. At Tweedmouth, however, the shelving shore allowed smacks and brigs to be beached, but more importantly vessels up to 400 and 500 tons could be accommodated at the Carr Rock. Two railways existed (horse-drawn), one from

When this photograph was taken in 1900, Tweedmouth Docks were only twenty-five years old. A three-masted barque and a smaller brigantine are tied up on the western side of the dock.

A map of 1828 showing the railway from Unthank Colliery to Tweedmouth.

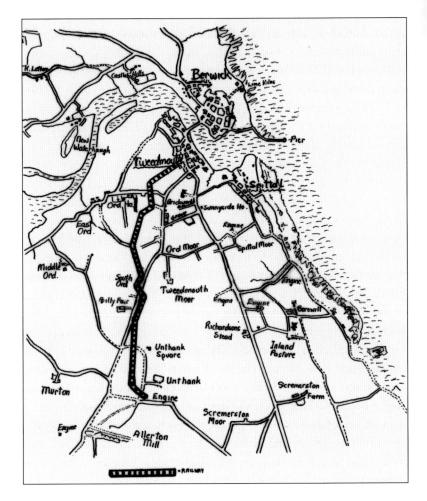

Unthank coalmine in Ord to Tweedmouth for the carriage of coal, and similarly a railway from Scremerston to the coal jetty at Hallowstell, Spittal.

In Tweedmouth there was a tannery and, in the West End, tile sheds for the manufacture of pantiles. At the East end, Robertson and Guthrie's iron foundry made amongst other things lamp posts (which were exported to India), in the process using large quantities of water from St Cuthbert's Well. There was a soap manufactory, also a pipe factory making clay tobacco pipes, the pipe clay probably coming from the south west of England by ship, to be unloaded on Tweedmouth strand. There was also a brewery.

The salmon fishing stations on the south side of the river below the bridge were the most profitable, some years previously being worth £2,553, compared to only £700 on the north side. Herring houses were springing up in both Tweedmouth and Spittal and at the latter, the boats could discharge their catches on the shelving shore adjacent to the herring curing yards.

There existed in Tweedmouth as early as 1806 a four-storeyed mill where three pairs of milling stones were powered by a 12hp steam engine, 'one of the greatest curiosities that ever we had in this place', according to James Good.

This picture of prosperity is mirrored in the number of taverns in Tweedmouth and Spittal in the 1820s, and their names give clues as to the occupations of the populace: Blacksmith's

Arms, Foundry, Harrow, Plough, Salmon, Pitman's Arms, Ship, Smack and Boat. The Harrow stills exists today, as does the Boat, now a private house but with its internal bar furnishings still in place. Whether these taverns sold smuggled whisky is not known, but it must have been popular for in 1832 a petition was raised by the people of Berwick addressed to the House of Commons, complaining about the high incidence of smuggling from over the border. This had 'demoralized its population, depressed its industry, and increased its public burthens' – the latter referring to the large number of smugglers being detained in the local gaol at the townspeople's expense.

Certainly Spittal had a large number of people engaged in smuggling and Sir Walter Scott writing in 1832, told of the two nations (England and Scotland) having different laws (hence the lower duty on spirits in Scotland), and he gives a graphic account of one Spittaler by the name of Richard Mendham. He was a carpenter who rose to opulence, although he could neither read nor write. 'He found means to build in a suburb of Berwick called Spittal, a street of small houses as if for the investment of property. He himself inhabited one of these; another, a species of public house, was open to his confederates, who held secret and unsuspected communication with him by crossing the roofs of the intervening houses, and descending by a trap stair, which admitted them into the alcove of the dining room of Dick Mendham's private mansion.' In the stable of Dick's mansion, a post of one of the stalls could be turned which gave admittance to an underground vault which held the contraband goods. Richard Mendham was tried and executed at Jedburgh when Sir Walter Scott was present as Sheriff of Selkirkshire. Even today in one or two of the oldest houses in Spittal, there are concealed underground 'hidie-holes', which no doubt were useful for concealing the illicit spirits. In addition to the goods smuggled between Scotland and England, other contraband goods would be landed on Spittal's beach from the Continent, including French brandy and claret, also cases of tobacco and boxes of tea. These would be swiftly despatched inland by pack horse, where a ready market awaited.

Further up the coast at Eyemouth, two merchants in the style of Richard Mendham built the large mansion house of Gunsgreen from the profits of smuggling claret from the Continent, but they were lucky and did not pay with their lives as did poor Dick.

The Thatch Inn, prior to its burning down in 1886. At one time, punch bowls and ladles used by the workmen building the Old Bridge were kept in this tavern. The mounting block shown can still be seen today outside the present Thatch Inn.

To the right of the large building with the bay windows, is a group of three old houses, reputedly the properties of Richard Mendham, smuggler and counterfeiter. These buildings were bombed during the Second World War.

Perhaps all this cheap booze affected the Spittalers' senses, for at this time, one public house was called the Elephant, a strange name for it is doubtful if any residents would have seen such a beast – perhaps it should have been Pink Elephant! A few years later, the minister of the Presbyterian church in Spittal was writing: 'We have a greater proportion than I have seen or heard of in any village, of very aged, infirm, lame, maimed, drunken, dissolute and very poor persons', and he blamed the former smuggling practices.

Poor Spittal did not even receive a good notice in the *Guide for Passengers using Berwick Smacks*, published in 1824. 'The village that stands upon the southern bank of the Tweed, at its very mouth is Spittle. This is almost wholly inhabited by sea-faring people, who not infrequently convey in their boats, tourists and parties of pleasure to Holy Island. They used to be reckoned of peculiarly unaccommodating dispositions and boisterous manners.'

Sometimes uninformed people speak distastefully of the name Spittal, and certainly, it was at one time spelled 'Spittle'. However it has an honourable origin in the medieval Latin word 'hospitale' (or hospice), the Hospital of St Bartholomew for the care of lepers being founded in Spittal before 1235. Various lands were endowed and gifted for the upkeep of the hospital, which was sited in the area of what used to be Spittal Hall Farm between the bottom of the Billendean Road and Dock Road, adjacent to the Brandy Well and the Billing Dean Burn. There was a mill which ground the corn from the hospital's fields and the brethren were given the right to fish for salmon at the fishing place adjoining their land, hence the present day name of Hallowstell (Holy fishing place).

There was a tower for defensive purposes because of raids by the Scots, also a house for the master, and small detached houses or huts for the lepers. This leper hospital eventually became a place for poor people, as the scourge of leprosy died down in the fourteenth century. Subsequently, through various grants and purchases over the centuries, it became Spittal Hall Farm, and during the Second World War when the farm buildings were derelict, they were set on fire deliberately for a practice fire brigade exercise.

Some 400 years after the hospital of Spittal ceased caring for the poor and diseased, people again began to come looking for a cure. By 1800, the spa water of Spittal was claimed to be one of the finest mineral waters in the north of England, and many cures were claimed among the poor 'who have been affected with a leprous or scorbutic humour in the blood'. This claim

*Hallowstell Fishery
closed in June 2001
after 1,000 years of
continuous history.*

may well have had foundation in fact, for the maladies described are in the nature of scurvy, which sometimes results from anaemia caused by iron deficiency. That the chalybeate waters of Spittal contained copious amounts of salts of iron can be attested to by the author, for as a child the spa water appealed so much he became unwell by partaking of it too freely! In 1885 it is suggested in Dawson's guidebook that infants be not allowed to drink more than ten pints a day as 'we hardly think it would be beneficial'! The water, drunk from a heavy iron cup attached to a chain, meant some enfeebled invalids might have struggled to lift the cup to their lips, such was the combined weight of the cup and chain! Alas, both the old well higher up on the hillside and the new well

*The old spa well, when
the highly regarded
chalybeate waters were
still flowing.*

(both situated behind the War Memorial) have been dry for half a century or more, and no doubt they would not be allowed to function today on the grounds of public safety. It must be said, however, that the present day tap water, though it may have purifying chemicals added for our safety (e.g. chlorine), does not taste as good as the spa water did.

Spittal, of course, had the added attraction of sea bathing both from the beach and also in the sea-water baths offered by the likes of J. Burn, proprietor, Windsor Cottage, Sea Road, in the 1880s. Open from 6 a.m. to 10 p.m., a hot bath was 1s, a cold bath 9d. The sea water was pumped directly from the foreshore ensuring that customers had the benefits of the salt water, while not having to endure the lack of privacy and the cold which prevailed in beach bathing.

The local newspaper recorded visitors to Spittal, and in the early nineteenth century one such was the eleventh Earl of Buchan from Dryburgh. He came for a month complete with his family and retinue of servants, residing in one of the larger houses built in Spittal for that purpose. He it was who caused the massive monument of William Wallace to be erected above Dryburgh in 1814, which it was stated, could be seen from Berwick before trees surrounded the statue. The Earl lived until he was eighty-seven, so perhaps his holidays at Spittal and the Spa water can claim some credit for his longevity.

One who achieved an even greater age was a Mr John Park who moved to Spittal when his employers (Black's Spade Works) moved from the forge at Ford to Spittal in 1855. He worked for Blacks for sixty-five years and died at the age of niney-five.

If visitors were valued in Spittal, as they were, bailiffs certainly were not. In 1859, Monday 10 October had been stormy, and this had prevented the white fishers from leaving the harbour. The red fish (i.e. salmon), however, had come into the river in large quantities due to the storm, and practically the whole of Spittal turned out to engage in poaching. Eight boats for poaching were manned, and were supported by the populace on shore, all armed with stones, many with slings. They not only drove thirteen water bailiffs back to Berwick, but gave chase, captured the bailiffs' boat and sunk her. As the local paper reported: 'The men [i.e. the poachers] were disguised in their wives' bedgowns, and there is likely to be some difficulty in identification.'

Robert Elliot's blacksmith's shop in Sandstell Road, Spittal, c. 1907, in the days when horse power was supreme and the blacksmith was essential to the economy.

CHAPTER 8
Shipping

In the twelfth century, David I, King of Scotland, designated certain towns to be the only places where buying, selling, and manufacturing could take place. It was a form of protectionism, but the main purpose was to grow these burghs, increase revenue, and most importantly, to attract foreigners who would bring their knowledge and skills. Berwick was the largest burgh in the south, being the main port, and as such it became the wealthiest burgh in Scotland. It ranked with Ghent, Rotterdam and other great cities in the Low Countries, and was almost the rival of London in mercantile enterprise. Many of the early merchants who were attracted to Berwick came from Flanders and Northern France and became burgesses. They were allowed special privileges in trading and Berwick was a bustling sea port handling freight. There were shipyards, warehouses and associated trades such as sailmakers which would be clustered in the area where the ships berthed. Berwick thus had a strong maritime tradition in its golden period of prosperity.

In the middle of the eighteenth century after centuries of stagnation, Berwick's maritime trade began to stir once more and Arthur Byram was sufficiently attracted to establish a shipbuilding business below Berwick Quay. He and his descendants built first-class ships for over a century, and Byram is credited with the design of the fast sailing ships which have a unique reputation in maritime history – these were known as Berwick smacks. Originally designed to provide a speedy delivery of Tweed salmon to the London market, the Berwick smack was developed further, until it became primarily a large passenger ship offering fast transit from Berwick and Leith to London. The average voyage took three to five days, but one passage was completed in the record time of 44 hours,

A lithograph done prior to 1825, for it shows the ornate bridge gate which was removed in that year. On the left is depicted a rather small Berwick smack, while on the right, a paddle steamer crosses the river.

An aerial view of 1985 showing the shipyard slipway, also the area of Palace Green and the Ness.

these times contrasting strongly with the much longer stagecoach journeys. A shipping company was formed in 1764 by local men, mainly coopers, who had salmon fishing rights, and this company eventually became the Berwick Salmon Fisheries Company, which only ceased trading (after two and a quarter centuries) in 1989. In their hey-day twenty-one smacks were providing a regular service between Berwick and London, and in addition Berwick smacks were being operated out of Leith by Leith traders, who had set up their own company. Goods were transported on the smacks as well as salmon and passengers, while other ships such as brigs carried more cargo than passengers. With the development of turnpike roads, Berwick became as the hub of a wheel with its spokes radiating out to towns in the Scottish borders, and to a lesser extent in north Northumberland. Barley, oats, wheat, eggs, potatoes, wool and leather were shipped from Berwick, and the return voyages brought goods and passengers destined for Berwick and the Borders. It was said that ladies in Berwick were dressed in the most up-to-date fashions, due to the quick and easy passage of goods and information from London.

The men who sailed on these ships were tough, resourceful, and skilled in their craft, none more so than the skippers, one of the most notable being Jeremiah Ward, Captain of the smack *Tweed*. He was widely thought to have sold his soul to the Devil in return for which he would always have advantageous winds and currents. This belief seems to have been widely held, and details of his uncanny prowess are written about in *A Trip in a Berwick Smack*, a book published in 1815. Among his papers in the Berwick Archives is

The Ceres, *a Berwick smack of 1797 in full sail. The tiny figures give a good idea of the scale of these fast ships, which could take passengers from Berwick to the heart of London in 44 hours.*

his hand-written remedy for a pain in the side, breast or back: 'Enough gunpowder and lump sugar pounded that will sit on a shilling. Take it at fasting with a glass of gin or whisky.' As the three components of gunpowder are saltpetre (a diuretic) sulphur (a laxative) and carbon (expels wind) it would appear that with such a potion, any lesser person than Ward would have required no assistance from the Devil as regards wind! Ward's gunpowder would be easily obtained, for all smacks were armed with cannon as a defence against privateer ships, which often attacked them when voyaging to London.

The smacks, though, were expensive to build and maintain, for the huge amount of canvas required some ten or eleven seamen to manhandle it. Clipper schooners superseded the smacks, and two of these, the *Tweed* and the *Teviot*, were built by Gowan at Berwick. These were renowned for their speed and it was not unknown for a clipper schooner to do the trip from Leith to London in 33 hours. The *Teviot* took part in a race from Archangel to London against an Aberdeen ship, the agreed prize for the winner being a long hat for the skipper and a tripe supper for the crew. The *Teviot* won easily! Another ship built by Gowan, which literally sailed round the world, was the *Border Maid*, a forerunner of the beautiful clipper ships which still excite the imagination, when the Tall Ships Race takes place round our shores.

Other shipyards were in existence in the early nineteenth century; one, adjacent to the south end of the old bridge was operated by Joseph Todd, who had been a cooper. He built two man-of-war brigs for the Admiralty, the larger being HMS *Rover* of 382 tons, with sixteen carronades (cannon) and two 6lb guns. Both ships saw successful action in the Baltic against Danish ships during the Napoleonic wars. Todd became bankrupt in 1808 so perhaps Admiralty work was less than profitable.

Another venture at this time was the establishment of a whaling fishery, and two Berwick ships, the *Lively* and the *Norfolk*, sailed to the Greenland waters, hunting the Greenland right whale up until the 1830s. Number 1 Wellington Terrace was the home of a director of the whaling company, and the panels of the front door still display harpoon head decorations.

A large barque lies at the end of the Carr Rock pier, c. 1887. It is square rigged on two masts, and fore and aft on the rear mast.

The *Norfolk* was trapped in the ice during two seasons and on one homecoming, a large part of the population of Berwick turned out on the walls and quayside to cheer and welcome it home after its long absence. One cooper who worked on a whaler used his earnings to good account when he started a herring curing business in 1847. This was Robert Boston, whose firm became one of the biggest in the herring trade and lasted for 100 years, until the dearth of herring and changing eating habits brought about its demise.

WALKING TOURS

A Walk Round Berwick's Elizabethan Walls

A convenient starting point for this 1 ½ mile walk is the car park at the bottom of Castlegate (where there are toilets). Pass under the nearest arch of the Scotsgate, and turn left up the Cockle steps under an arch which may have been the original Scotsgate Arch. This was moved to its present position, when the gate was widened in 1815. A few yards on the left is a flight of steps which takes you to the higher level of the ramparts. You are now on the Elizabethan town walls, built according to Italian military design by Sir Richard Lee between 1558 and 1565. A complete circuit can be made of the walls, crossing only one road, with the spire of the Town Hall acting as a pivotal sighting point.

Proceed to the left until you are standing above the Scotsgate Arch.

Looking south is the Marygate, and at its foot is the Town or Guild Hall, with its imposing 150ft spire. In the distance is the coastline, with its castles of Bamburgh and Lindisfarne. Looking north you will see the Castlegate, i.e. the street leading to the Castle.

Carry on across the Scotsgate and climb the steps to Megs Mount, which is signposted.

On this bastion a cannon once stood named 'Roaring Meg'. From here there are splendid views looking up the Tweed valley towards Scotland, with the triple peaks of the Eildon Hills 35 miles distant. Looking south across the river with its three fine bridges, are Tweedmouth and Spittal, and beyond are the Cheviot Hills.

Descend the walkway towards the arches of the Royal Tweed Bridge.

On the right is a statue of Lady Jerningham whose husband was a Member of Parliament for Berwick in the 1880s. Further on and

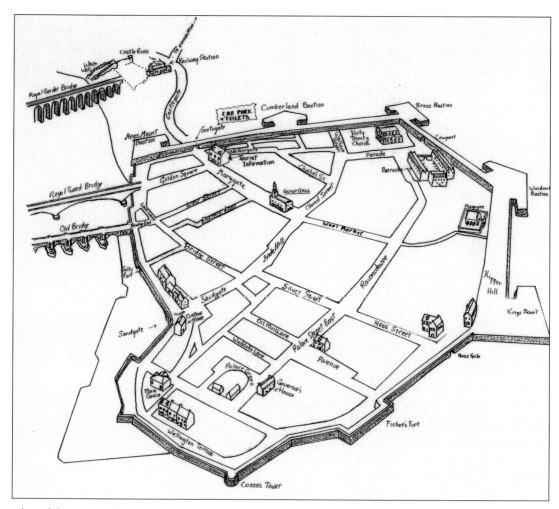

Plan of the present-day
town, showing main
reference points.

*Berwick Marygate,
c. 1895. On the extreme
right is the Salmon Inn,
and next door, Hogarth
the butchers. Outside
Hogarth's a butcher's
boy with a striped
apron, holds a horse's
head, no doubt for a
customer in the shop.*

**Walking
Tour**

looking upwards on the left is the 200-year-old building of the former Corporation Academy where freemen's children were educated. It is now the Leaping Salmon Inn. After passing under the bridge, the entrance to an ice house can be seen on the left. This was where ice gathered in the winter or imported from Scandinavia was stored, and used for preserving salmon sent to London in the eighteenth and nineteenth centuries in the famous sailing vessels, the Berwick smacks.

Continue towards the Old Bridge to Bridge End, where there are seats.

This is where there was a gatehouse guarding the bridge entrance to the town. The bridge, built on medieval lines with pointed cutwaters and piers, is nearly 400 years old, being the fifth bridge to have been built across the river near this point, covering most of the last millennium. Also in this vicinity was a small hospital and chapel known as the Maison Dieu (House of God), founded in the thirteenth century, which looked after the spiritual and physical needs of travellers. Looking left you will see the building where the firm of Cowes (established 200 years ago) still make the traditional wholesome sweets known as Berwick Cockles. It was this view that L.S. Lowry famously painted in 1935, looking towards the Town Hall spire and including the 'Home of the original Berwick Cockle'. Lowry was very fond of Berwick and from the 1930s to the 1960s was a frequent visitor, spending many holidays here.

Now cross the road – watch for traffic from the left.

As you proceed, the Georgian houses fronting onto the walls are worthy of attention. Built in the latter part of the eighteenth century for merchants, they command a fine view over the river, and behind them are some large granaries and warehouses, now converted for other uses. Looking down on the Quayside and small harbour, one can imagine the merchants surveying the ships as their cargoes were being unloaded. Now there is no mercantile bustle, nor as in the later years of the nineteenth century are there herring fishing boats six deep unloading their catches. In the summer there are sailings from the quayside, a boat taking passengers as far as the suspension bridge at Horncliffe. Enquire at the Tourist Office for details. From this quay in the middle of the eighteenth century, the fast Berwick smacks took

Walking Tour

An auction of agricultural machines outside the Corn Exchange, which at this time (1900) was one of the principal exchanges in Britain.

passengers directly into the heart of London on a regular twice-weekly service.

> **Walking on, you will come to the Sandgate, or Shoregate.**

You are now standing above an entry to the quayside. Looking into the town, on the left is the Playhouse Cinema which was formerly a granary. On the right is the Hen and Chickens Hotel, which was a coaching inn in the eighteenth and nineteenth centuries. Beyond the Hen and Chickens is the former Corn Exchange, which was one of the foremost grain exchanges in Britain.

Looking to your right along the walls is the Customs House (No. 18). This handsome building in the Adam style was a merchant's house, with a huge warehouse beneath, which adjoins a cavernous ice house. A few yards further on, No. 21 has the distinctive and attractive Venetian style of windows, and in this house lived an artist of some repute, Thomas Sword Good (1789-1872). Painting local scenes and people, his style was akin to the famous Scottish painter David Wilkie.

> **Carry on until you come to a sloping cobbled walkway on the left.**

At the foot of the walkway is the Main Guard. This originally stood in the Marygate and housed the guards of the walls and gates, but was removed to its present position in 1815. In the summer months, interesting exhibitions are staged here by the Berwick Civic Society.

> **Return to the walls and continue along Wellington Terrace.**

Here three houses are grouped together. Number 1 has the harpoon decoration on its door as described in Chapter 8. Opposite these houses are positions for thirteen cannon, and at the point where the walls turn north is Coxon's Tower. Built to defend the walls from sea attack by guns placed on the upper gun deck, it has on a lower level a fine rib-vaulted storage chamber.

Proceed northwards to Nessgate.

You will pass the Four Gun Battery and then Fishers' Fort with six emplacements which overlook and guard the river. Until the Second World War, cannon stood at all the gunports, but now there is only one, of a later date – a Russian cannon captured in the Crimea.

Stop above the Ness Gate (an opening made in 1815 to provide a road to the new pier) and look towards the rise in the walls. You are looking at part of the medieval wall with one of the semi-circular towers which still remain. These towers (of which there were more than fifteen) were built at regular intervals along the walls (see the 1745 map of old and new fortifications). This one, the Black Watch tower, would originally have been much higher, being reduced in height in the fifteenth century. Beyond the tower is Kings Mount, a half-bastion, and from this point on we will be walking on top of the Elizabethan Ramparts back to our starting point.

Walk up Kipper Hill towards Windmill Bastion.

The name Kipper Hill is derived from the old kippering houses on the left, now restored and converted into private housing. After the path has levelled out you will notice on the left the Magazine where gunpowder was kept securely for the garrison. The buttressed building and surrounding walls were designed to contain any explosion.

Windmill Bastion is signposted and is so named because of a windmill sited there in the sixteenth century. This is a good point to look north along the curtain wall between the Windmill and Brass Bastions, both pointed like arrow heads. Their flankers (gun recesses at ground level) could give covering fire to each other along the front of the curtain wall, and also the faces of the bastions. You will notice the huge earthen mounds on top of the bastions – these were gun platforms from which cannon could fire down and give all round covering fire. The Windmill Bastion was used as a coastal defence battery in the second half of the nineteenth century, and during the

Walking Tour

Walking Tour

last war anti-aircraft guns continued its defensive purpose.

In front of Windmill Bastion is a man-made mound triangular in shape, known as the Great Bulwark in the Snook. Defensive in purpose, it preceded the Elizabethan Walls. Also to be seen looking southwards are the remains of a rectangular fort or citadel, the building of which was curtailed by the construction of the Elizabethan Walls.

Continue to Brass Bastion.

Half-way along you will come to the Cow Port, the only original gateway in the walls, built at the end of the sixteenth century. It is worth descending to street level to see the wooden doors and, under the archway looking upwards, you will see the recess where the portcullis was held, ready to be dropped. Outside the gate (or port) was a bridge over the moat, the ditch surrounding the walls being filled with water. In the middle of the moat (200ft wide) was an especially deep ditch with an 8ft drop, for any unwary attacker. Continue to Brass Bastion and from the top looking north, remains of the old Edwardian walls (started in the thirteenth century) can be seen. Also visible is the octagonal Bell Tower built in the sixteenth century to replace an earlier one. In that area is also the remains of an artillery fort, Lord's Mount, built in the time of Henry VIII before the construction of the Elizabethan Walls.

On the west side of the bastion (above the recessed flanker) is a cobbled sentry walk, and looking down, the exit of a tunnel can be seen – this gave access to the flanker from an entrance near the parish church. This bastion has the dubious distinction of sometimes being referred to as Devil's Mount, for Satan is supposed to appear to anyone who walks round it three times at the witching hour.

Conclude your walk by continuing to Cumberland Bastion.

This bastion was originally known as Middle Mount but was renamed in honour of the Duke of Cumberland who defeated the Jacobite forces at the Battle of Culloden in 1746. It has a seventeenth-century gun in the flanker placed to show how the angle of fire along the walls would deter any attacking force. The area adjoining this bastion was for many years used as a cattle market. Now return to the Scots Gate, your original starting point.

A Walk inside the Walls, from the Town Hall

The Town (or Guild) Hall situated at the foot of the main shopping street, the Marygate, is open to the public – see the notice at the north side entrance for times etc. It is well worth a visit, for in addition to the main assembly rooms and council chambers, there is on the upper floor, the former town gaol. The cells are as they were when built in the 1750s, and there is a comprehensive and interesting display of photographs and artefacts. Graffiti on the cell walls date from a time when convicts imprisoned there awaiting transportation to the colonies filled their miserable hours by incising outlines of boats and even the gallows! Sentences of life transportation were common, and from the condemned cell, death awaited felons on Gallows Hill (near the present railway station). The last public hanging was of Grace Griffen in 1823 who was found guilty of murdering her husband.

Street markets are held in the Marygate on Wednesdays and Saturdays under the provision of various Royal Charters dating back more than 700 years.

Proceed up Marygate, going into West Street, the second street on the left.

This cobbled street has some good shops and descends quite steeply to Bridge End. At the bottom, turn right along Love Lane for 100 yards. An open courtyard on the right reveals at the back some

The condemned cell in the Town Hall gaol. When the door is shut the cell is in total darkness. In 1823, the unfortunate Grace Griffen was the last person to be hanged at Gallow's Knowe, and she spent her last miserable hours here.

Berwick smacks figure prominently in the incised graffito on the walls of the gaol in Berwick Town Hall.

Walking Tour

Substantial buildings, the doors of which would have given access onto street level hundreds of years ago, still exist today below the pavements of Bridge Street.

steep walls, part of which is the ancient Cat Well Wall, built about 1562. This was designed to shorten the length of the walls by leaving out the lower part of the town. It was never completed, however, as the garrison store-houses would then have been fatally outwith the walls. Here also was the Ravensdale priory which had its origins in the thirteenth century, and in this area beneath some of the pavements and buildings, are substantial remains of earlier constructions, which have been covered by subsequent heightenings of the street level over the centuries.

Retrace your steps to Bridge Street.

This is one of the most interesting streets in Berwick, being possibly the oldest. Today it still retains its historic feel with its narrow alleyways and passages through the walls, and huge leaning eighteenth-century granaries. In old guidebooks there is mention of cellars with mooring rings on their walls, suggesting that before there was a quayside, the river was much wider than it is today. The interior of William Cowe & Sons' grocers shop (Nos 64-66) is a fascinating reminder of more gracious days, when one was served by an experienced grocer when buying provisions. Further along on the right is the Sallyport. As its name implies, this was for soldiers moving quickly through the walls to resist an attacking force. Go into the passage under the walls and look for the change in masonry, which shows where the Edwardian wall was enclosed within the Elizabethan Wall. On the other side of the street is Shoe Lane, with a sign above the entry. At one time in the Middle Ages, hundreds of men were engaged in shoemaking, and in this courtyard is one such shoe factory, dating from the nineteenth century. The building has now been converted to dwellings. Also in this courtyard is a timber-framed building of the early eighteenth century.

Bridge Street today has an interesting mix of services, which range from health food shops to a model shop, and lovers of antiques, books and photography are also well catered for. Near the end of this street stood the Red Hall, the headquarters and trading post of Flemish merchants who were slaughtered in 1296, when Edward I took and ravished the town.

Emerging from Bridge Street, cross Sandgate and enter the small street opposite the cinema.

Walking Tour

This leads you into the Palace Green area where there was a Friary dating from the thirteenth century, possibly that of the Carmelite order. Certainly an extensive group of buildings is shown on a sixteenth-century map, enclosing a courtyard with an elaborate fountain. This area was known as the Palace, and it is likely that the friary became the seat of the King's administration after the Dissolution of the Monasteries in the 1530s.

On the east side of Palace Green is the Governor's House, built in 1719, where the military governors of Berwick had their residence. At one time the governors had swingeing powers, but by the nineteenth century the office of governor was a sinecure, and it was finally done away with in 1833.

In this area is the Main Guard already mentioned in the previous walk round the walls; also in Palace Street West there are seventeenth- and eighteenth-century houses. In Palace Green the wall of a house on the north side displays a fire insurance mark from the eighteenth century. In the event of fire, if a house had this mark it was assured of help from the town fire brigade.

Leave Palace Green by Palace Street East, on the north side.

On the left is Avenue House, built in the eighteenth century, which displays a coat of arms. Behind this house, in a yard off Weddell's Lane, are fragments of medieval stonework complete with a royal crown. Opposite is The Avenue leading to the Walls. This area was the site of a ropery which explains the long unbuilt-on area of grass. At the end of the Avenue, is a brick-built house, The Retreat (built 1740), which still retains much of its original interior features. Moving on, No. 5 Palace Street East (on the right-hand side) was originally a mansion house, then the Grammar School, and now it is the Community Centre.

Turn left into Silver Street.

On the left-hand side beneath the car showrooms are extensive cellars, sometimes used for exhibitions and functions. With beautiful brick arching and pillars, the cellars were formerly used by the Berwick Brewery for the storage of beer and wines. Somewhere near this area was another monastic site, occupied by the Austin Friars, and it is tempting to think the cellars may have had an existence before the date shown over the cellar entrance (1781).

Holmes, fishmongers and salmon merchants, Bridge Street, Berwick, in 1930. In 1310, a Ranulf de Holm, salmon merchant in Berwick, sold £9 5s 8d worth of salmon to the King.

Governor's House in Palace Green.

Walking Tour

At the end of Silver Street, turn right into Hide Hill.

Walking uphill, you will see on the right the King's Arms Hotel, a coaching inn from the eighteenth century. Here, stagecoaches bound for Edinburgh and London stopped to allow passengers a break for a meal, while the horses were changed over. In this hotel, Charles Dickens gave readings of his works when on his tours in 1858 and 1861.

Opposite is Popinjay's Restaurant, occupying part of a building erected by Captain Philips in 1718. Towards the top of Hide Hill on the right is the Brown Bear public house with a vennel at the side leading to the remains of a Presbyterian church. In its origins this church had associations with John Knox when he was a resident preacher in Berwick in 1549-51.

At the top of Hide Hill, by turning left you come to the rear of the Guild Hall. This part was built a few years later than the main building, and on the ground floor, old cells now house a shop and coffee house. The pillared open space, the Buttermarket, was in use up to the last century as a market for butter, eggs and poultry. Outside, there is a mounting block which enabled riders to climb on to their horses.

Leave Buttermarket on the north side and walk up Church Street.

Church Street, originally known as Sutergate (shoe-makers' street) has some attractive cobbled yards and vennels. In Berwick, churches were often discreetly tucked away behind the streets, and an arched entrance just beyond the police station led to St Aidan's church, now the Peace church. This was where the Dispensary once stood, which was the forerunner of the Berwick Infirmary.

Below the police station yard, the building with the Venetian windows was the old Cannon Inn, which now has only the undercarriage of a miniature cannon left of its old sign. Nearing the Parade, No. 57 on the left with its Venetian windows strikes an attractive note. A little further on, a brick-built house set back slightly, was built as the vicarage some 250 years ago.

Proceed to Holy Trinity parish church.

Walking Tour

Looking diagonally across the Parade, where soldiers used to march, is the Holy Trinity parish church, almost hidden by the churchyard trees. It is an unusual building and unique, for it is one of only two churches that were built during the Commonwealth under Cromwell, Lord Protector. Built in 1650-52, next to the site where the medieval church stood, most of the building material was stripped from Berwick Castle, which had been purchased by the Guild expressly for that purpose. Severely classical and practical, it has no spire, such adornments being frowned on by the Puritans. Nevertheless its interior is pleasing to the eye with its columns, arches and Venetian-type windows. There are some interesting roundels in the west window of early Flemish origin, and in the south windows, two charming roundels representing Morning (Aurora, Roman goddess of the dawn and her cherub of light) and in the other, Night and her children, Sleep and Death. The reredos is by Lutyens and there are some interesting monuments, including one to the initiator of the church, Colonel George Fenwick, who was Governor of Berwick and Oliver Cromwell's friend. From the sixteenth century onwards, the *Book of Common Prayer* has always singled out Berwick, stating in the preamble that it was to be used in all cathedrals, universities and parish churches within the Kingdom of England, Dominion of Wales and town of Berwick upon Tweed! The pulpit is thought to be Elizabethan, and there is a long-standing tradition that this is the pulpit John Knox preached from. Happily it is now re-united with its tester or sounding board. The missing tester was discovered recently by the Vicar, having been cut in two halves, doing service as bracketed shelves! There are some interesting gravestones in the churchyard including one for Arthur Byram, the master shipbuilder (see Chapter 8).

Cross the Parade to the Military Barracks.

Do not be put off by the rather forbidding entrance to the Barracks, with its heavy gates. There is a charge for admission, but inside there are three interesting and separate exhibitions and museums. There is The Kings Own Scottish Borderers Regimental Museum; the English Heritage History of the British Army (By Beat of Drum) and the Berwick Borough Museum with its history of the town in 'A Window on Berwick'. Upstairs in the town museum are two galleries of paintings and artefacts gifted by Sir William Burrell who lived at Hutton Castle six miles from Berwick.

The Barracks themselves are still used by Army Cadet and Air Training Corps units, thus continuing its long military history.

Berwick Castle and the White Wall. The White Wall was built by Edward I in 1297 to provide safe access from the castle to the river, and as a defensive work. The tower at the base of the wall extended further into the river, and at one time, provided a landing point for ships and supplies for the castle.

Walking Tour

The sixteenth-century Bell Tower sitting on the line of the Edwardian walls of which some remnants are seen adjacent to the tower.

The Constable Tower was at the south-east corner of the Castle and dates from the late thirteenth century. It can be seen from Castle Vale Park (entry from Station Yard).

Completed in 1721, the Barracks were the first purpose-built barracks in Britain. Prior to this, great discontent was fomented in the townspeople who had to accommodate soldiers in their houses and inns, often with little or no recompense. It was thus with great relief that soldiers of the garrison, numbering up to 700 men, could be safely contained within the confines of their barracks.

On two nights in September, a splendid military tattoo takes place in the Barrack's square. This should not be missed if you are in Berwick at this time.

Other Suggested Walks

Walk to the lighthouse at the end of the pier, with access through the Ness Gate and along Pier Road. Grey seals are often in evidence at the river mouth, hunting for salmon. ($1\frac{1}{2}$ miles there and back)

A riverside walk commences at Love Lane (leading off Bridge Street). This goes under the Royal Tweed and Royal Border Bridges up to the Castle fortifications, which extend down to the river with a stepped defensive wall known as Break Neck Stairs (correctly the White Wall, built 1297-98). Pass through the White Wall Tower and continue along the path to a gate which takes you up Tommy the Miller's Field. From here the remains of Berwick's Castle can be examined. At the base of the wall where the facing stone has not been robbed, an indication of the castle's original magnificence can be obtained. Continuing to the exit gate at the top of the field, a grassy knoll on your left is Gallows Knowe where public hangings were carried out. Leaving the park, opposite is the old Toll House, and turning right you can return to the town by Castlegate with its individual and varied shops. A detour can be made into the railway station entrance where a gate on the left beyond the telephone box takes you into Castle Vale Park. From this path, a good view can be obtained of the thirteenth-century Constable Tower (part of the castle). You may continue down through the park, which will bring you back to the riverside for your return.

Near the railway station are direction signs for the Holiday Camp, and by following these you will be walking along the line of the old Edwardian Walls. The octagonal Bell Tower sits astride the line of the thirteenth-century wall fragments and ditch, and a little further on you can view Lords Mount, an artillery tower dating from Henry VIII's time. By continuing along to a fork in the road and bearing right you will cross the golf course, and come back through the Cow Port to the Parade and Barracks.

Walking Tour

Walk across the Old Bridge (built 1611-24) to Tweedmouth, and explore the area. There is a pottery at Tower House and a good variety of shops and restaurants, and some fine views looking across to Berwick. In the summer season, salmon fishermen can sometimes be observed with their distinctive cobles, netting salmon. Return via the modern Royal Tweed Bridge to Berwick town centre.

A pleasant walk along the promenade at Spittal gives rewarding views of Berwick Bay and Spittal's golden sands. If you wish to continue up on to the cliff path at the south end, this will take you to Sea House and Cocklawburn beach. Return over the level crossing to Scremerston and then back along the footpath on the old A1 to the roundabout on the outskirts of Tweedmouth. There at Bonarsteads, is the very fine Swan Leisure Centre with its excellent swimming pool and extensive range of sports facilities.

BERWICK-UPON-TWEED'S WAR WITH RUSSIA

The short answer is no! The long answer is that because of Berwick's unique position, the town was mentioned separately in Acts of Parliament, and it is a long-held tradition that when war broke out in the Crimea in 1854, the formal declaration of war included Berwick, but due to an oversight it was omitted from the terms of the peace treaty in 1856. To lend weight to the story, it is interesting that even as late as 1840, a patent for a form of daguerrotype photography was taken out by Richard Beard 'within England, Wales and the town of Berwick-upon-Tweed'. So, as this form of nomenclature was still being used in 1840, just fourteen years before the Crimean War, it is easy to understand how the story originated and how it has doggedly survived.

Is the Russian bear still fighting the one from the most northerly corner of England?

Leisure Pursuits

Details of the following attractions can be obtained at the Tourist Office, Marygate.

The Swan Leisure Centre with swimming pool and gymnasium, at Bonarsteads
The Maltings Theatre, Arts Centre, and Restaurant (access by Eastern Lane off Marygate)
Playhouse Cinema, Sandgate
Municipal golf course, Magdalene Fields
Goswick golf course (5 miles south of Berwick)
Bowling greens at Berwick, Tweedmouth and Spittal
Tennis courts at Berwick
Fishing trips
Museums at the Barracks, which includes the Berwick Borough Museum
Guild Hall   tours and museum
Lowry Trail – places in Berwick featured in L.S. Lowry's paintings
Street markets on Wednesdays and Saturdays
River Tweed boat trips

Places to visit in the surrounding area

Bamburgh Castle and Grace Darling Museum
Beadnell
Belford
Chillingham Castle (and cattle)
Etal Village and Castle
Flodden Field
Ford Village
Halidon Hill
Heatherslaw (working grain mill and restaurant, also narrow gauge railway to Etal Castle)
Holy Island and Lindisfarne Castle
Norham Castle and Church
Paxton House and Country Park
Seahouses (for boat trips to the Farne Islands)
Wooler and the Cheviot Hills

Index